WELCOME TO THE #UNARMEDFORCES

COMBAT
FLIP FLOPS

OFFICIAL MEMBER

Steps Ascending:
Rise of the Unarmed Forces

Printed in the United States of America
First Printing, 2018
ISBN 978-0-9992937-9-9 (ebook)
ISBN 978-0-9992937-8-2 (softcover)
ISBN 978-0-9992937-7-5 (hardcover)
Feral Productions

For signed copies visit www.Combatflipflops.com

To Estella and Amelia,
Without either of you, none of this would have been possible.
Thank you for being a constant source of positivity,
motivation, and love. Everything I do, I do for you.

To Michele,
Thank you for being on this adventure and the reminder,
"Whatever happens, it's the best possible thing that could
have happened."

To Lee,
Ride or Die. You exemplify hard work,
friendship, and family.

To Andy,
The best brother I could have ever wished for. As always,
"Think for yourself. Question authority."

To Leo,
Roses are red. Violets are blue.
Thanks for making this possible. Be you.

To the Unarmed Forces,
If we all do a little, together we do a lot. Please continue to
make a difference, no matter how small, every day. Because
there is only one way forward—together.

Contents

Foreword vii

Preface xvii

Chapter I - The Beginning 1

Chapter II - Before the Beginning 31

Chapter III - Social Relevance 45

Chapter IV - I Still Can't Think of Anything 67

Chapter V - Packing Boxes 77

Chapter VI - Garage Days 102

PART II: RISE 113

Chapter VII - Visions of White 115

Chapter VIII - Going Beyond 137

Chapter IX - Surfing with Sharks 145

About the Authors 161

Foreword

Afghanistan is a landlocked country wedged between Iran, Pakistan, and a few other "stans." It's known as the Graveyard of Empires because life in Afghanistan is so brutal that any army attempting to subjugate the people fall victim to the persevering nature of her violent conditions, then find themselves beaten by hardened and experienced Afghan fighters accustom to the environment. From all of the records in human history, the story stays virtually the same: an army invades, they become worn by the weather and the mountains, and then Afghans exploit their extended and weakened state to take their lives, guns, money, and food. The Maurya Empire of ancient India, Alexander the Great of Macedon, Umar, an Arab Caliphate, Genghis Khan of Mongolia, Timur of Persia and Central Asia, the Mughal Empire of India, various Persian Empires, the British Empire, the Sikh Empire, the Soviet Union, and most recently, a coalition force of NATO troops all know this ruthless truth firsthand.

In the 1950s and 1960s, Afghanistan was a neutral nation on the rise. The country progressed rapidly during the courtship by the United States and Russia during The Cold War). As a nation with a history of warfare, Afghans leveraged the battling superpowers to acquire Russian machinery and defense equipment and receive foreign aid from the United States. International organizations built roads through mountain passes to connect Afghans in a historic manner, burkas became optional, and education thrived in pursuit of a more prosperous culture.

In the 1970s that progress slowed with violent coups, civil wars, and the invasion of the Soviet Army in December 1979. The war started as the result of left-wing military officers overthrowing the centrist government. Afghans are typically independent, so the idea of a communist government didn't sit well with the population at the time. When the new government tried to purge opposing parties, it lead to the rise of the Mujahideen—"Those who engage in Jihad."

In an effort to quell the growing rebellion, the Soviets invaded Afghanistan with 30,000 troops, toppled the government, and installed a new national leader. The Afghans didn't dig that too much and mounted an insurgency rebellion backed by a foreign government across the Pakistan border. The Russians kept working to put down the rebellion. Their efforts peaked with over 100,000 troops in country, controlling large garrisons and major city centers, but they were losing miserably to the insurgents who operated with freedom of movement in the rural areas. Over time, muslims and anti-Soviet powers from all over the world poured across the Pakistani border to help the rebel Afghans. Russia lost over 15,000 soldiers and suffered the injury of many more, only to withdraw to a divided, broken, failed nation. Once again, Afghanistan became the Graveyard of Empires.

By 1989, the Russians withdrew from Afghanistan. The Afghan refugees were expected to return home to destroyed villages, tattered school systems, and a fractured economy, so it's not surprising that there were still roughly 4.3 million refugees in Iran and Pakistan. That's a lot of humans living in refugee camps in one of the world's toughest environments. It may be difficult for western minds to imagine the scale of such dearth. It's possible that our dictionary doesn't even contain a word to capture the pain, agony, and destitution to describe that level of extreme poverty. Millions of people suffer because two Western powers decided to fight over an idea of a ruling style of government—communism or democracy.

The citizens of Afghanistan responded in their historically successful manner. They let the foreign army invade, utilized the topography and weather to extend their foe, then crushed them over time with knowledge of the terrain, experience, and sheer grit. All of history proves this method to be effective. It's simple, inexpensive, and potent. No need to change the strategy when it works.

The Russian withdrawal left the Afghan economy in ruins. The educational system was non-existent. There was, however, no shortage of open terrain, guns, munitions, and international interests looking to position themselves in the country to make the most of the tragedy. A power vacuum ensued.

Between 1989 and 1996 Afghanistan was plagued with civil war and multiple shifts in governance. When the

Soviets left and the Americans quit backing the anti-Soviets, regional players stepped up to gain power. Although Iran and Uzbekistan ran operations in their own interest, Pakistan was the major player in the civil war. Skipping a bunch of history, the Afghans lead by Ahmad Shah Massoud held off the Pakistani-backed Gulbuddin Hekmatyar for years despite multiple ground assaults and rocket attacks on Kabul and surrounding regions. Ten years of costly warfare from Western powers over a conflicting idea about how goods and services should be traded was immediately followed by another seven years of internal strife. When Pakistan realized that Hekmatyar would never take Kabul, they devised a different plan.

While endless battles reduced Kabul to further rubble, a new radical ideology began to take root in the country. Mullah Mohammed Omar, a Muslim cleric, developed the Taliban movement by inspiring angry youth to take up arms and pursue violence to stabilize their nation.

The Taliban quickly captured Kandahar and advanced on Kabul. Pakistan's Inter-Services Intelligence (ISI) shifted its support to this culturally relevant group.[1] In far less time than the Russians or coup-driven forces could ever achieve, the Taliban was at the gates of Kabul and quickly gaining power. On September 26,1996, the Taliban invaded the UN compound securing Afghanistan's president, Mohammad Najibullah.

---

[1] http://www.mei.edu/content/post-soviet-pakistani-interference-afghanistan-how-and-why

In a display of power and violence, the Taliban shot both Mohammad Najibullah and his brother in the head, and then mutilated, castrated, and dragged them behind a truck through the streets of Kabul. Their bodies were hung on public display in order to show the public that a new era had begun—one marked with oppression, violence, and the return of Osama Bin Laden to Afghanistan.[2]

1996 to 2001 in Afghanistan was rough to say the least. Fighting continued between independent Afghans and the Taliban. When the Taliban took control of Kabul in September of 1996, they immediately implemented Sharia Law, severely restricting the employment of women. Seeing as most of the country's teachers were women, this led to rampant school closings. These school closures resulted in 3.7 million children 1, both boys and girls, without hope of obtaining an education. By February of 1998, home schools for girls, which had been allowed to continue at first, were forbidden. There is a cunning brilliance in making ignorance an official policy. The Taliban waged a successful campaign against knowledge and information, knowing that an ignorant and hungry population is much easier to control. There exists, the world over, a relationship between education and opportunity. The lack of both in Afghanistan during this period created a ripple felt as far away as Nairobi, Kenya, Tanzania, Washington, DC, and Manhattan.

Cities and towns that resisted control fell under the pressure of constant war and abhorrent violence. Thousands

---

[2] https://en.wikipedia.org/wiki/Mohammad_Najibullah#Final_years_and_death

of Afghan citizens were rounded up and executed, religious minorities forced to identify themselves with markings on clothing, and history wiped from their landscape. After years of fighting, a group of uneducated, angry youth gained power in a way that nobody expected, backed by those with experience and money, they executed tragedies that will be a stain on our species for all of history.

In October 2001, the US military invaded Afghanistan. In the seventeen years since, over 150,000 people have died, and over two trillion dollars, (that's $2,000,000,000,000) have been spent fighting an ideology birthed of illiteracy.

We've spent trillions on warfare and millions on education. Over the last two decades, children without access to an education dropped from 3,700,000 to 3,500,000. After all of that loss, all of those resources, we simply decreased the uneducated recruitment base by 200,000 youth, a 5.4% reduction. Most likely those youth were in urban centers near NATO bases. Armed forces kill countless "bad guys" in the rural regions of the nation, and yet more just keep taking their place. Why?

You know the answer. It happened in the same location and under the same circumstances twenty-two years prior and continues to happen all over the world every day. Organizations like the Taliban, al-Qaeda, Boko Haram, MS-13, and ISIS prey on the uneducated, disenfranchised, and unemployed. They use despair, anger, and frustration to incite young men to violence as a tool to gain power.

The majority of the country's population simply can't read. I'll say it again. They can't read. They can't write. They can't interpret the words written in the single book from which they are governed, a book frequently distorted to draconian ends. They can't bring their thoughts and hopes for the future into reality. Limitless defense spending, smart bombs, or troop surges won't change that.

We can no longer claim ignorance. Moving forward with the same course of action now means we are either too full of pride to admit our mistakes, or so morally bankrupt that we simply need to feed the military industrial complex, waging endless war in search of profit. Neither of those answers, by the way, are historically sustainable.

There are currently 3.5 million potential replacements for every "bad guy" the military takes out, and more are born every day. As a matter of fact, the infant mortality rate in Afghanistan has decreased by 42% since 2001.[3]

Literacy rates have increased 5.4%. Infant survivability improved by 42%. If you're not getting the math, the population of uneducated youth destined for violence mathematically outpaces educated youth every day. As a global population, we are living the analogy of cutting the head off the Hydra. For every one head we cut off, two take its place. This is the simple math of our reality.

Let that sink in.

The previous pages were intended as an abbreviated history lesson to show the cyclical relationship between destruction and illiteracy. A cycle which results perpetually with angry, uneducated youth leveraged into violence. If we

---

[3] https://data.worldbank.org/indicator/SP.DYN.IMRT.IN?locations=AF

really want to break the cycle, we must empower the population from within with employment and education. In doing so, we enable the youth to bring love into their world.

The first step to solving a problem is being aware it exists. The next is taking accountability. Most people are aware, or at least I hope they are aware, that the United States has been engaged in a protracted war in Afghanistan for close to two decades, making it the longest war in the history of the United States, a nation that has been engaged in war 222 of its 239 years (93% of its existence). However, that isn't even necessarily the problem, per se. The problem is actually more in the way we, as a global community, engage in that war.

This really smart human named Albert Einstein is attributed with saying, "No problem can be solved from the same level of consciousness that created it. You must learn to see the world anew." I understand the challenge in this. It requires a person to step away from their own vault of human experience and see the world from the perspective of a person or group of people whom they've likely never met. This requires significant reflection, awareness, and empathy, which are tactics not traditionally utilized or even considered when it comes to winning wars. As Einstein also said, "Insanity is doing the same thing over and over again, but expecting different results." We've used copious bombs and bullets to solve a problem essentially initiated with bombs and bullets. It may be time to depart from the costly insanity and try a new approach.

Over the past two decades, nearly one million Americans have fought valiantly in Afghanistan against the wrong enemy. Our guerilla adversary lurking in the shadows is not a religion, a political group, or a way of life. Our enemy has always been ignorance and desperation—two things you can't defeat with a bullet or a bomb.

Our world leaders waged war on an ideology, using fear as a recruitment tool. Terrorism. Terrorist. Terror. Terror. Terror. Everywhere. A fluid concept to be manipulated as time passes to keep the cogs of war turning profits for social and political elites while coalition corpses, juiced up on altruism, are draped in their nation's flag.

If we must kill, let's kill ignorance. If we must wage war, let us wage war on poverty and desperation. The deadliest weapons in this war are knowledge and information. Education is the empowerment that ultimately triumphs oppression.

Without functioning companies, there are no jobs. No jobs means no income and no payroll taxes. No taxes means no schools. No schools means no educated workforce to employ in companies to pull the country out of poverty. No profit means no education and no jobs. Both the chicken and the egg have gone rancid.

How does a nation with a fractured economy create the profit necessary to generate a tax base to provide its citizens with an education that will allow them to feed the positive growth cycle? Allow me to answer the question with another question.

What if funding for schools in the most deserving and

necessary parts of the world could come directly from or be supplemented by for-profit business? What if part of that business model simultaneously activated that same underutilized workforce?

Preface

There's a special moment of the day I particularly love. It has a heavy feeling in my hand and smells like the heat rising from the first sip of fresh black coffee. The desert air is damp, almost cool. There is a stillness over the ocean. My daughter's dreams play out their final scene. Her head still heavy on the pillow. The sound of nothing echos through the open air of the home I built.

The phone rings. *What? My phone never rings. There's only about a dozen people who even have my number.*

"Hey, Leo. You wanna write a book that sells a million copies? Become a famous author?"

"Griff, buddy. I've worked very hard my entire adult life to not be famous. Fame is a fool's game."

"Okay. You wanna write a book that puts hundreds of girls in Afghanistan in school?"

"That I might bite on."

"I have an opportunity. My company is going to appear on Amazon's main page as a featured business on cyber monday. Since we found out, we've spent everyday preparing. We've leveraged every opportunity and created as much product as we possibly can. Even with all our preparation, the truth is, we are going to sell out completely within a few hours. I need a product that can't sell out, Leo. I need a book."

"Wow. That's huge, buddy. Congratulations."

"This is a massive opportunity to push the mission forward."

"Wait. Cyber Monday? Griff, haha. That's in three months. Is the manuscript complete."

"What? No, Leo look. I need you to write it."

"You want to write, edit, format, design, and publish a book in ninety days? Haha. Griff, buddy. That timeline is absolutely insane."

"Leo. Do you remember what we used to do for a living? Come on."

"If it was anyone else on the planet, I would have hung up the phone already. What is the book about?"

"That's up to you. I was thinking of calling it, Don't Try This at Home."

"Wait, you don't even have a concept? So we need to conceptualize, write, edit, format, design, and publish an entire book in ninety days? Griff, the book process typically take anywhere from one to three years to complete. The editing process alone typically takes more than three months. A book is a marathon, not a sprint. It's foolish to run a marathon at a sprint pace. You never make the finish."

"Leeeeoooo."

"This is crazy. This entire conversation is crazy. How are your girls?"

"They're doing great. Estella is crushing…"

Admittedly, this was a stall tactic on my part. I needed a moment to think. *Is this possible? If so, how? What would the tone of the book be? What would be the message? What would be the first sentence? I'm already writing two other books right now. I've always supported Griff's mission. I believe in it. This is a chance to do good in the world using my particular skill set. Ninety days. What the fuck, ninety days.*

"Oh man, that's awesome to hear. Hey, how much creative control do I have on this project?"

"Total. You're the artist, man."

"First, your title sucks. Sorry, but I see your business as something that people should at home. I think you're right, a book would be a great force multiplier for your message in so many ways, none more so than encouraging other entrepreneurs to follow your lead. *Steps Ascending.* It makes sense. Footwear. Rising up. Ah, um elevating. Beyond. Being, um. Hey, I gotta go. I need time to process."

"You do you, buddy. Love you."

I smeared wax on a dinged up 5' 8" fish from the quiver of surfboards in the corner of my bodega and walked barefoot the half mile to the beach. The waves were small. Perfect size for thinking. Forty-five minutes later, a mental rough draft was organized in my mind. It could be done. It would be brutal, but it could be done.

"Okay, Griff. We can do this. But you are writing this with me. And when it comes to writing books, good is not good enough."

"This is going to be so much fun."

"I've gotta get to work on this immediately. I'll be in touch."

"Love you, buddy."

"Do not follow where the path may lead, go instead where there is no path and leave a trail."

-R.W. Emerson

Chapter I
-The Beginning-

There is ease in familiarity. This time, familiarity is framed in a new and unsettling way by the tiny double-paned window descending rapidly over the jagged snow-capped, war-torn mountains below. Those mountains used to feel scary, violent, uncomfortable to the sight. Truth be told, they're no less scary, violent, or uncomfortable now. Perhaps I've just learned to better appreciate them after years of fear and admiration.

The padded reclining coach seat and tray table, now in their respective full and upright positions. Seat belt securely fastened. A different view of the same place. A different perspective from the crowded cargo net of the cramped C-17 military transport aircraft of days long past.

We're on a standard flight pattern. In from the West, fly over the city, make a northward loop over the Military Training Center, and then land on an East-West heading. These morning flights are always special. Sun peeking up over the horizon, the smoke from the cooking fires mixing with the ever-present dust that blows in from any one of the dry valleys surrounding the city. Sharp rays of light pierce the smoke, completing the otherwise ominous scene with eerie beauty.

I always try to sit on the left side of the plane to see if I can catch a glimpse of the Great Wall, sometimes referred to as the "Wall of Bones." It's over 1,000 years old and has survived countless wars. The wall was built to funnel invaders off the hillside and into the valleys for easy killing, and it stands as a reminder: *Invaders beware. We'll build a huge fucking wall up a steep-ass mountain just so we don't have to walk up there to kill you.*

Welcome to Afghanistan.

The armrest between Jasmine and I is covered in duct tape. She is new to the group. We'd met in person for the first time in the Dubai main terminal only three hours earlier. Brown hair peeked out gently from under her headscarf, atop crystal blue eyes and a warm smile at the blessing of full lips. The rest of her five-and-a-half-foot frame is covered in fashionably baggy, earth-toned attire that shows she is working to be respectful to the local culture. Months earlier, a mutual marketing friend recommended her via Skype. For reasons unbeknownst to me, Jasmine thought it was a good idea to tag along on this adventure. She paid her own way on a trip to an active war zone. I hope she doesn't die.

Under-inflated wheels aggressively punch the tarmac, announcing to the limited space between my lumbar vertebra that we've landed. The left side of the runway is populated by several eras of aviation history. Russian planes. American Planes. French helicopters. Some were running, others were scrap. But there they sat, a tribute to the international effort in Afghanistan. Millions of dollars of equipment sitting idle, decaying. But look at all these new helicopters and planes on the north side of the runway. They'll get it right this time.

Whenever traveling, it really doesn't feel like I've arrived until the plane stops and the seatbelt light goes off. We've arrived. And regardless of nationality, race, or religion, everybody wants off the fucking plane. Afghans, contractors, diplomats, and our newly formed team of four all stretch overhead toward disheveled bags in the overhead compartments before beginning the slow shuffle to the door.

The stairs are wheeled to the side of the plane, like we took off in 2012 and landed in 1975. With ridgid strides, we advance toward the anachronistic, single-story terminal. The first thing that hits you here is the smell. The odor drags me immediately seven years into the past. The mix of dust, wood fire, shit fire, plastic fire, and whatever other kind of fire is being used to heat homes and cook food this morning, and every other morning for thousands of years, hangs in the valleys around Kabul. Imagine the best campfire you've ever smelled, then throw ten plastic bags and a dried turd onto the coals. It's like that, and it makes me feel twenty-four years old again.

We're out of place in the most obvious of ways. None of us are covered in tattoos, overly muscular, or militant in appearance. Three white guys and a white girl in civilian attire entering the baggage claim at Hamid Karzai International Airport.

After a few minutes of chaos, yelling in multiple languages, and hiring a baggage dude, we have all of our bags

3

on a cart and stand in the customs line. There is a universal quality about customs officials the world over that makes you feel like you've done something wrong, even when you haven't. All the passports are in order: Fresh visas, documentation from our Afghan business partners, and a letter of invitation from the US Department of Commerce. Still, I'm nervous. Step to the counter. Meet his cold stare with a warm smile, pass the documents, and wait.

Stamp, stamp. Stamp, stamp. Stamp, stamp. A little ink along with an emotionless head nod up and to the right and it appears we've been allowed entry. The stoic man slides our paperwork back across the counter, and our team advances. It pays to have your shit together.

Out of the madness of the airport and into the wild of war. Because the security threat is so high, vehicles are not permitted to pull up to the airport terminal without special clearance. Passengers are met by counterparts on the ground. It is easy to pair them together visually. The muscular, tacti-cool guys on the plane are met by an equally or greater tattooed guy with just as many or more pockets on his pants. Standard loose-fitting, plaid, button-down, to "conceal" the pistol holstered on a standard gun-belt. They immediately start giving each other shit while lifting molle-covered nylon bags over their shoulders. They're on their way to do one thing—make money. Tough to blame them; there's plenty of the stuff being thrown around. Difficult to tell at the street level where the people live, of course. There are plenty of days in which that path seems more logical than my current journey.

Diplomats are met by, well, diplomats. Athletic but thin looking Americans in their mid-twenties. It's difficult to know if they actually care about the mission or if they just took the posting to look good on the resume and sound even better in a bar. Nice shoes, nice slacks, pressed button-down shirt, trimmed hair, and the cool-guy aviator glasses. How are these guys so clean? I can never remember being that clean in country? And rarely do you see Afghans that clean. But there they are. Hygienic, well-kept American diplomats picking up fresh faces to fill desks behind large blast walls.

As for us, there's nobody there to meet us in the terminal. We have to make our way to "M." M's name is going to stay private, as he served as a Special Forces interpreter for several years and now works in the private sector. By his Facebook profile and the pictures shown to me by a trusted Green Beret, he looked big. Bigger than most Afghans. As close to 200 pounds as he was to six foot. Fresh haircut. Solid jaw. Definitely looks like he's not to be fucked with. Plus, he was recommended as a trustworthy counterpart by proven fighters. Good enough for me.

The four of us in a tight pack, bags over the shoulders, moved toward the door. I'd done this walk a few times before on previous trips. Exit to the left and make the 100-yard walk to an opening between the blast walls. Afghan military guards stand at the entrance to check passports on the way in. We pass by on our way out. Behind the walls is a parking lot full of armored vehicles. Contractors load into Land Cruisers, the diplomats into armored vans. It's a flurry of conversation, lifting, and the choke of diesel engines firing up.

Past the blast walls on the other side of the parking lot is the civilian entrance. More military guards stand at a large opening with hundreds of Afghans waiting for friends and family to arrive. As we approach the crowd, the nervousness begins to set in. The other members of the team maintain a silent confidence in my ability to link us up with a reliable contact on the ground.

Man, I hope he's here.

Andy turns and asks me, "Is he in the crowd?"

"No, he said he'd meet us in the parking lot."

We press forward down the sidewalk, pass the garden, and turn right into a single-story building full of restaurants and gift shops. The smell of flatbread and grilled meat fill the building. We aren't stopping for kebab. Straight through and out into the parking lot full of taxis and dilapidated white Toyota Corollas.

Pause. Look. Breathe. Scan. Calm in chaos. There he is. M. Thank God.

There's a saying in business and in the military, "Amateurs talk tactics. Professionals talk logistics." It doesn't matter how fast you run, how far you can shoot, or what objective you're going to slay, it doesn't fucking matter if you can't get there without adequate rest and enough food—and back.

Afghans, despite all the negative things said in the media, are huggers. They aren't afraid of a heart-to-heart embrace between two beings. No armor. No barriers. A warm introduction to show that you're in this world together. Without hesitation, M steps up. "Nice to meet you, brother." A handshake, hug, and smile.

After a brief introduction, the bags are loaded into the back of the Corolla. This car is just how I want it: old, dented, a few swipe marks, and covered in dust. It blends right in with the hundreds of others in the parking lot and on the streets of Kabul. We aren't carrying guns or wearing body armor. Our best defense against the IEDs and attacks is to simply blend in. Before they notice you're there, be gone in the mix of traffic with little defining features to identify your vehicle.

Things seem to come in threes. Logistics revolve around sleep, chow, and transport. We have one of the three covered, and now it's time to work on the other two. It's a fifteen-minute drive into town, hit the Massoud Circle, then head east down Jalalabad Road. With the help of Gerald, a former Army Sergeant Major, we'd reserved four rooms in a secured compound off the beaten path and away from diplomats and big security contractors. Time to make the run.

Andy is 220 pounds of hard-working Montana rock, stacked six and a half feet up. Stylish black leather shoes, seersucker pants, jet-black button-down business shirt, big goatee, black rectangular glasses, and neatly trimmed hair you would expect from any West Coast businessman. He's too big to fit in the back seat, so he gets to ride shotgun. Jed behind Andy, Jasmine in the middle, and me in the seat behind M.

It's a straight shot out of the airport to Massoud Circle. I fucking hate this drive. It's known for grenade attacks, gunfire, and IEDs. Contractors, diplomats, and rich people have to take this route out of the airport. It's easy pickings for anybody wanting to drop a gringo or ten. The route is constantly patrolled by police and military, but that doesn't make me feel any better.

It's a familiar sight, numb to me due to the past six years of travel in developing nations, but Andy, Jed, and Jasmine remain wide-eyed to the tumult occuring on the other side of the Toyota's cracked windshield. The road is full of potholes and lined with dirt access roads filled with stands, donkey-pulled carts, police cars, and poverty.

Afghan traffic circles are a miracle. They're a fluid mass of cars, carts, bicycles going multiple directions, and noise. As we slow going into the circle, a little girl raps on Jed's window and gives the international hand signal for money. It's always heartbreaking to see children out on the street. Are her parents alive? If they are alive, why isn't she in school? Where does she live? Before the questions quit, the car rolls into the circle at twelve o'clock and out at three o'clock, heading east.

The directions are fairly easy by local standards. Head east on Jalalabad Road until you see the big green gas station. Turn right before said gas station. The gate is one hundred yards down on the left. Simple enough.

There's the gas station. Turn left, and there it is. A twenty-foot-tall wall with a big metal door in the middle. On either side of the door are towers with AK-toting Afghans inside. Looks like our place. As we roll up to the gate containing our security, food, warmth, and coffee, we survey the surrounding territory. Across the street, a commonplace scene tells the story of Afghan poverty. A rock-covered field adorn with plastic bags whipping in the wind. In the foreground, a ditch filled with human feces. There is a small, single-story home immediately adjacent. The front of the home has mounds of dirt with small brown patties laid across the mounds, facing south.

She's been quiet up to this point, but Jasmine finally inquires, "What's that?"

"It's shit," I reply. "They flatten fecal matter into patties and dry it out. It burns enough to heat the home and cook food."

Jasmine's facial reaction well represents a person with limited experience in a developing nation—one who lives in the abundance of modern-day New York City.

It's full participation at this point. "Breathe deep."

M honked in front of the gate. I call ahead to Gerald. They are expecting us. The door crepitates to the left. We slowly roll in.

There's a rule when operating in conflict areas: "If there is any doubt, there isn't any."

The security protocols are the same for everyone, regardless of nationality or the number of times you've passed through the giant metal door to the blast containment area. Once we cross the threshold, the metal gate closes behind us. Concrete blast walls extend up to the left and right. A serpentine arrangement of concrete blast walls in front prevent vehicles from advancing forward faster than a crawl. If we were loaded with explosives and decided to pop one off, the force of the explosion would push against the blast walls and up skyward. The metal gate would likely be trashed as well. This is life in Afghanistan. There are no doubts. Everyone is suspect. Everything is checked.

Uniformed Afghans wearing body armor and toting rifles enter the containment area and signal us to exit the vehicle. M already has his documents in hand. We exit the vehicle, M and me from the driver's side, everybody else on the opposite. M and the guard go through the paperwork. Jasmine, Jed, and Andy appear as curious as they do exhausted. This is likely their first time in a concrete cell.

A working dog, some European breed likely sold by a contractor, specifically trained to sniff out varieties of explosives, moves in a clockwise pattern around the vehicle. *Man, I hope M wasn't doing anything around guns with the car in the past week.* Approximately a minute later, after inspecting all sections of the car, the dog and trainer disappear back behind the wall. M, papers in hand, shuffles back into the car. We're in.

Our vehicle slow-rolls over crunching gravel through the zigzag pattern of blast walls. Zig right. Zag left. One more zig to the right and straight into the open parking lot. Row by row of twenty-foot, white containers, stacked two high, with exterior stairs on each end. Air conditioners pump cold air into the base of the buildings, semi-covered by Afghan rose bushes.

The war effort has been great for the container industry. Take a container, plumb a bathroom into the far end, wall it off, then stick a bedroom in the front. Wire for power.

Bam. Instant living space for any service member or contractor. The arrangement of containers in this compound makes up a twenty-unit building. Five containers are lined up, then stacked two high. An equal stack of containers built opposite of them. A small hallway with a door on the end joins the two stacks. Exterior stairs give residents access to the upper hallway and rows of containers. The arrangement is perfect. Stack as many containers as possible without giving the buildings a shooting angle for rockets or RPGs over the blast walls.

An athletic American woman in her mid-thirties meets us in the parking lot to assist with check-in. The process of checking into a hotel, at its essence, is the same everywhere you go; some paperwork, exchange of cash, a quick tour, security brief about potential threats and recent suicide bombings, location of dining facility and gym, and a set of room keys. She points us to our container and returns to her office with just enough time for our group to make the final minutes of breakfast.

For the most part, chow halls are the same the world over. A stainless steel bar with a tray rack along the front. A plastic sneeze guard protects pans of colorless vegetables and overcooked meat from unwanted aerosol attacks. Grab your tray, slide down the line, quickly select your desired caloric intake so as to not impede the flow of hungry traffic on this single-lane, one way street. Big coolers akin to those at most American gas stations house selections of soda, milk, yogurt, and non-alcoholic beer, positioned evenly along the wall. A table to the right displays hot water heaters, stacked coffee cups, and tubs of Nescafé. Nescafé. The nectar of Asia.

After two full days of traveling, an eleven-and-a-half-hour time zone change, and the stress of movement through Kabul, the meal-time conversation of our group fell a bit flat. Add a belly full of food, and none among us were a match for the dominating force of the impending food coma.

We haul our bags up to the second story, enter our container-lined hallway and match the numbers on the door to the numbers on our keys. The room decor meets the expectations set by the architectural ambiance of the compound. Basic desk featuring a basic lamp. Single bed with hotel-style bedding. Armoire on the left. Door to the rear leading into the bathroom. Sink, toilet, shower, and a few rough, white towels. Everything we need and then some. The final touch of comfort is palm sized- an off-white air conditioner remote control.

Traveling beyond familiarity is an opportunity for self-expansion, which is a cornerstone of self-improvement. In foreign environments, it is often necessary to slow down, to be more present in an effort to achieve the same tasks we are able to accomplish with ease and in a state of autopilot while at home. These rewarding challenges come in many forms, from language barriers to traffic laws to unfamiliar food choices. For the most part, I'm grateful for every one of these opportunities, but the fact that it damn near takes an advanced mathematics degree to accurately convert Fahrenheit to Celsius is an enigma beyond my capacity to appreciate. So I dial the number down to the remote's lowest limit, chirp it back up a few clicks, and hope for the best. As

I lie down for a quick nap, I find comfort in knowing that since 1969 the moon has only ever functioned in Fahrenheit.

BEEP, BEEP, dzzzzzzzzz, BEEP, BEEP, dzzzzzzzzz…

What the f—Where am I? Why am I so tired? Light switch? Stumble. Touch. Reach. Fuck, I hate this feeling. Stumble a little more. There it is.

Shit. I'm in a container in Afghanistan.

The air conditioned room lured me quickly into a deep, comforting sleep following the long, strenuous movement. The arrogant rattling vibration and obnoxious tone of the cell phone on the basic desk pulled me back even faster.

We have several afternoon meetings scheduled. It's time to get to work. I hope the team was able to get some rest.

The door swings inward into the container. All I can hear down the hallway is Jed's deep voice. "Low'r yer F-stop."

Jed's room is across the hallway and down three doors. I peek around the corner. Jed is holding up his Nikon as Jasmine stares at the screen. His fingers fly around the camera to manipulate all the settings. The mix of photography technical terms combined with his southern drawl sounds like a foreign language, perhaps due to this sleep deprived state. The only thing recognizable is the repeat of, "Lower your F-stop." It must be crucial, as he keeps reiterating the advice over and over to her, as if it is the fundamental basis of good photography.

Jed is a dapper Kentucky gentleman, standing a shade

13

under six foot. He looks every bit the part of a professional outdoor photographer. Active pants, wrinkled short-sleeved, button-down shirt with pockets in the front, two days of travel stubble, and disheveled hair that somehow still looks unbelievably fashionable tells the story of a man experienced in the art of austere. We met a year earlier at the Outdoor Retailer Show in Salt Lake City. He did catalog photography for a few companies in the industry, and we met through mutual friends while standing in line for beer. We quickly became friends over our love for hunting. Now he sits there at the end of a twin bed, teaching a fashionista how to use his big-dollar gear.

Jed's job on this trip is to capture video. The adventure is almost too unbelievable to be true, so we are recording everything to quell any doubt. Part of Jasmine's role is to take photos. She's been behind a camera before. Now with Jed's tutelage and continued encouragement to "Lower your F-stop," the trip will have plenty of quality documentation.

We have two meetings for the afternoon. The first is with the Task Force for Business and Stability Operations (TFBSO). The TFBSO is a Department of Defense (DoD) organization that started after the Iraq invasion and was transplanted to Afghanistan. TFBSO founder and former deputy under secretary of defense Paul Brinkley described TFBSO once, stating, "We do capitalism. We're about helping companies make money."

A like-minded organization to ours, no doubt.

Within the hour, all four of us are back in the gravel parking lot, loading into M's Corolla, this time with a much lighter load. A lightweight camera bag holding Jed's Nikon and lenses sits in his lap. Jasmine has a large purse with her camera inside. Andy and I look somewhat stupid, as we carry the same Arc'teryx laptop bag in two different colors. We maintain the same seating arrangement as our ride from the airport and give M directions to the TFBSO house in the diplomatic corridor of Kabul.

We exit through the blast containment maze, through the big gate, and attempt a left turn onto Jalalabad Road. In an ode to *Zoolander* fashion, the left turn is impossible. Kabul's afternoon traffic is so overwhelming that we can't cross the road and make the left to head west. Instead, M hangs a right down the service road just shy of the wave of Afghan traffic heading east. We bounce passed the standard developing nation storefronts—shipping containers. The large metal doors are wide open to reveal the goods on the inside of the small shops while the art of bartering occurs out in front.

Convenience Store. Propane store. Fabric Store. Convenience store. Candy store. Motorcycle repair shop.

"Stop the car! Stop the car right now!" I urge M. Aggressively, he smashes the wide pedal into the old floorboard, bringing us to a surprisingly immediate standstill.

The unexpected action draws a concerned look from each of my teammates. I'd forgot that they're still less than twelve hours into their first Afghan experience. Their expressions suggest something dangerous is about to happen, every possible negative scenario playing out rapidly across their eyes.

The bikes.

To our left are three custom Afghan motorcycles. Afghans ride small displacement Asian motorcycles that nobody's ever heard of in the United States. They're simple, fuel efficient, and Afghans have the ability to ride them anywhere while balancing a family, a refrigerator, livestock, or whatever they need to move to survive.

Even though most Afghan bikes are modes of transport or are used to earn a living, they come stock with an abundance of style. They are commonly decorated with multiple mirrors, colorful lights, tassels, and eccentric decorative paint. Color, texture, and style. Three elements that look great on camera.

"Jed, let's go get some photos with those guys and their bikes."

"What?" Jed replied.

"Those bikes, right there. They're fucking cool. Let's go get some photos with those guys and see if they'll do a photoshoot with us later this week after we pick up our gear. M, can you translate for us?"

I can only imagine what the Afghans are thinking when we pile out of the car. Andy towers at 6'6" and is in dress clothes, Jed wields a camera, Jasmine's blue eyes contrasts with her earth-toned attire, and a hippy looking guy wearing dress pants and a checkered shirt making the hand and arm signals to the Afghan bikers to take photos. That hand motion where you make a "C" out of your left hand, as if focusing a lens, the index finger of the right hand pressing and imaginary shutter. You know the one I'm talking about.

The world mirrors back to you what you express into it. Years prior, this interaction would have gone much differently for me. It would have been in the dark, my friends and I would have been armed to the teeth, and there wouldn't be any smiling. During those times, the world mirrored back equal darkness. This is going to be different.

Smile. Open heart. Be positive and authentic.

"M, can you tell these guys that their bikes are cool? And ask them if we can take their photos on these bikes. And as odd as it sounds, ask them if we can come back in a few days with our products and have them model them on the bikes for Jed?"

Americans have asked M to do a lot of things. Not sure if this is the oddest thing he's ever been asked to do, but he does struggle a bit finding the words to translate. He steps up and relays the request. The Afghan mechanics give us the standard suspicious stink-eye. Then one of them slowly walks over, and in the manor of enthusiastic hog owners the world over, starts to show us parts of his bike. It's on.

A few minutes of back and forth, photos snap of the Afghans staring in amazement and making gestures at Andy's size, and we are loaded back into the car and off to meet with the TFBSO. The team laughs about the randomness of the first interaction, which fills us with a feeling of good things to come. We are on our way to meet capitalists who help people make money.

Within moments, I realize that I've just set a frustrating precedent for M. As we enter the crammed Massoud Circle, Jed barks from the back seat, "Stop the car. I have to shoot this."

To our left, two Afghan boys each hold six foot sticks dripping with multicolored balloons. Each balloon is hand painted with contrasting colors and designs. The immediate assumption is that Afghans have kids too, and parents in the market will buy distractionary devices to keep them occupied while they shop. These children, however, are capitalists of their own accord. Ballon hustlers.

We all recognize the crisp purity of the moment from a photographer's standpoint. The scene is perfect. The sun hangs right over the tops of the cement buildings and blast walls; cars in the circle stir up dust. The rays of light from the setting sun shine through the ballon. The balloon hustlers are thin, stoic, dust covered, and bleeding texture from every conceivable angle.

Jed exits the car in a state of photographic flow. M does the translating, but Jed is already in the quintessential photographer crouch—bent over at the waist, camera body glued to his face, and hands in fluid support position. Andy and I have worked with professional photographers before, but this is a little different. He's lost in it. Years of experience and training puts him in this traffic circle to catch this moment. His left hand moves in semicircles on the lens, and his right hand resembles a spider on the shutter and camera settings.

It doesn't take long for the police to arrive. M lets them know that we are taking photos and will be gone in a minute or two. At that moment, an Afghan shouted in English from behind the hustlers. "You Americans are just using us. Taking images of poor kids for your own benefit." He doesn't sound happy.

There are plenty of rule number ones floating around—cardio…always look cool…people first. When operating, my rule number one is different: If there is any doubt, there isn't any. If something can go wrong, it will. Take action immediately to address the threat/risk/challenge and get ahead of it.

The immediate feeling of doubt set in.

"Jed, we're done here. M, time to go. Can you please give these kids some cash for allowing us to take pictures?"

The team knows what that means. Without a pause, Jed brakes his photographic flow and starts heading to the vehicle. In less than a minute, we're all back in the Corolla and moving into the great Massoud Circle amidst a hundred other identical cars, cutting seamlessly through grand-scale organized chaos.

Time to go meet the people who help capitalists make money.

Kabul resembles the urban terrain of many capital cities, with the big buildings in the middle. The structures get shorter and less valuable as you get farther from the interior. In the center of Kabul's hub are the foreign embassies. Obviously, the US embassy is the biggest. No traffic allowed within a block. Traffic checkpoints are covered by heavily armored vehicles with machine gun turrets on top, and layers of blast walls sit between the general population and the caucasian diplomats.

The embassy is the hub for all international interaction: defense, aid, security, finance. Although it's big, it can't house all of the staff required to run these operations. The military stays in the adjacent Camp Eggers or a NATO base. Aid, security, and finance staff stay in beautiful Afghan compounds in the adjacent neighborhoods. We are headed to one of these compounds.

Real estate is at a premium in Kabul. Tight dirt streets are lined by twenty-foot cement walls, most of which have another ten-feet of chain link fence extending above the barrier. The chain link is then covered by a green mesh material that piques Andy's curiosity.

"What's with the chain link and the mesh?"

"It's an RPG fence. People tend to fling a lot of rockets into this area of town. The additional ten feet gives them a tough line of sight into the compound. The mesh makes it tougher to spot when people are outside the buildings. You know, in case somebody feels froggy and wants to take a shot at a group of gringos. Plus, the fuse from the rocket goes off when it hits the chain link. This makes the rocket explode farther away from the building. You may get hit with shrapnel, but it's better than getting blown up and hit with shrapnel."

"Oh."

As we zig and zag through the diplomat and contractor neighborhood there's a mutual subtle urgency to get where the fuck we are going and be done with these broken roads and stale air trapped inside the tiny vehicle.

Every fifty to 100 feet stands a large metal gate leading into a compound, many of which are adorned with stacks of leaking sandbags and armed security. Others feature ominous guard towers behind their walls. Either shit goes down in this neighborhood often, or the people behind the walls have something valuable to protect. Either way, all five of us are on alert.

"This is it. Walk from here," M states casually as the Corolla rattles to a halt. He stays in the car as Jed, Jasmin, Andy, and I make the short, exposed walk to the TFBSO compound. Although we are a car laden with a fashionista, a photographer, a translator, and business owners, we easily could have been carrying explosives.

Names from here on out are changed to respect the security of the organization and to prevent any embarrassment of people working to make a change.

There's a standard song and dance when entering a compound in Afghanistan on foot. Make your way through a small access door to the left or right of a large metal gate. Instead of entering directly into the compound, step into either a cement or metal containment area to be met by two to three security team members. Hand over identification. Place your bags on the table to be searched. Hold your arms out to the side to be frisked. Although inconvenient when you're in a hurry, it is a necessary process and provides an iota of solace that's non-existent on the other side of the wall. Once cleared, one of the security guards bangs on the exit door which is opened by another guard on the inside of the compound.

We're in. It looks like every other urban Afghan building we'd raided in the dead of night a few years prior, yet it's altogether different. Much more alive in the light of day. Behind the gate, there's a cement driveway big enough to park three to four vehicles. Gardens and fountains line the space adjacent to the parked cars. Grapevines and flowers climb purposefully up the otherwise dismal walls. A massive entranceway sits atop a short flight of a stairs, twenty feet wide. The two-story Afghan architecture wrapped in decorative bricks, window facades, and bright colors snaps contrast to the compound's bleak curbside appeal. The steps are slow this time—ascending, purposeful, observant, not requiring a sprint toward the entrance in hopes of avoiding gunfire.

Our contact, Z, stands at the top of the staircase. We'd been introduced via email three months prior though a Department of Commerce contact. He's the TFBSO point of contact for small businesses looking to work within Afghanistan. There was a $5,000 investment for each team member to get to this meeting. Airfare, compound fees, food, M's day rate, and all of the other expenses involved with a trip to Afghanistan adds up to a $15,000 bet on a belief that we can make an impact.

TFBSO in Afghanistan concentrates on attracting private foreign direct investment, corporate development, procurement, and reform of the banking sector. Their budget is rumored in the five hundred million dollar range, of which we're attempting to secure a small fragment of. We've already demonstrated commercial success, have experience in country, and have a story that makes all parties look like rock stars.

There's Z. He is a lot younger than I expected. Maybe late twenties. Six feet tall with a wiry build, like a cross-country runner who spends his off time in the deployment gym. Exceptionally nice shoes, designer jeans, and a pressed collared shirt with the cuffs folded back. The cherry on top is the sunglasses—square aviators. He might as well have stepped out of a movie screen. He looks like every cliché CIA agent in a war zone, but cleaner and more stylish.

Seriously, how the hell do these guys stay so clean?

"Z, great to meet you. Thanks for taking the time to meet with us. We're excited to learn more about what you're doing for business here in Afghanistan."

"Great to meet you, as well. But before we get started, we have to get up to the cafeteria. It's fajita day. Don't want to miss that."

Andy and I quickly look at one another in amazement. *Fajitas?*

"Thank you for the offer, but we just had lunch and have another meeting to attend this evening. Any chance we can go through the brief and talk business?"

"I'm not kidding, guys. The fajitas are amazing. You have to have some. We can do the meeting in the cafeteria."

The mental image of a huge pile of money being set on fire flashes before me as my guts sink to just below knee level. This is pointless. Another government employee getting paid a stupid day rate in country to have meetings and put together slideshows. Fuck.

When I turn around, Jed is shoving his camera back into his bag, muttering through his smile with his Kentucky accent, "Guess we're not getting any work done here today."

Even the cameraman knows it.

"Ok. We have an important meeting with our manufacturer in a few hours. We have to arrange to pick up our product in the morning. Let's do the meeting in the cafeteria."

Z's mood picks up instantly as he spins toward the entrance. We walk up the stairs to the second floor and into a large room with a few tables with standard government seats placed around them—leather chairs backed by square chrome tubing. It's funny what's familiar to you when you step into a room. Sometimes there is also discomfort in familiarity. We're about to spend the next hour in these uncomfortable fucking chairs listening to a litany of clichés and playing MBA catchphrase bingo as it relates to development work. The room smells like a mixture of industrial floor cleaner and bastardized Tex-Mex cuisine.

And the universe gives birth to the "Fajita Lunch." From that moment forward, any meeting described as a "Fajita Lunch" means, "We thought this was going to be a mutually professional meeting between competent professionals. Instead, it's a bunch of highly paid individuals wasting time, repeating what they learned in school, unwilling to take risk to move forward, and noncommitment on any topic." The Fajita Lunch.

We discuss introductions, meetings, and access to people who "may" be able to provide capital for production. Yeah, right. In my head, I'm drawing the BINGO columns and filling the squares with "capacity building, facilitation, empowerment, foreign investment, etc." The blocks are practically scribbling themselves out as fast as I can come up with the words I've heard in dozens of government meetings and memos.

Jed ate a fajita. He's an avid athlete, Ironman, and backcountry hunter. His habit of onboarding calories when possible is predictable and impressive. Of course Jed was going to eat a fajita. For what it's worth, I'm happy someone got enjoyment out of the meeting.

After thirty minutes and no commitment or offer for help, we started angling for the door. Folding laptops shut, closing notebooks, and placing business cards on the lunchroom tables. Then it dawns on me that we flew all the way to Afghanistan and didn't even get enough respect to have a meeting in a meeting room. We got the cafeteria. With fajitas.

I thumb a quick text on the burner phone to M that it's time for pickup. He quickly replies with the five minute warning. Time to go.

"Z. Thank you for your time. If you can make any of those introductions for investment partners or manufacturers, please send them to my email. I'll be off and on internet over the next few days, so I'll respond as quickly as possible." Every person in that meeting knew full well there'd be no emails.

Standard handshakes and smiles all around. Back out through the checkpoint gate. M is 200 yards down and to the right. As soon as he sees us exit the gate, the Corolla fires up, and the lights come on. He quickly executes a five point turn in the tight street so that we can approach from the rear. The team enters in our standard seating arrangement. As soon as the car doors close, Andy poignantly gives summation of the meeting. "Fucking fajitas! Are you fucking kidding me? Fucking Fajita Lunch," he states, in a manner backed by twenty years of experience as a professional construction manager, a profession which demands keeping a lot of the bullshit you see to yourself. But every now and then somebody comes up with something so new and so stupid that it can't be contained, even with two decades of experience. He is pissed, which is a rarity for as long as I've known the man.

In his earlier years, he wore hair down to his ass and his beard to his belly button. Standing at the height of the average NBA player, he resembled everyone's favorite intergalactic pilot, Chewbacca. That look earned him the name "Wookie." It's fitting. When shit's going wrong, he starts yelling, banging on everything in site, and all of a sudden, life pops into warp drive. It's magical to watch. Lately, he's been banging spreadsheets, sketchup designs, and wire transfers.

"Let's get our heads on straight. We're headed to meet John and Eli. M, do you know where the Gandamack is?"

"Yeah, boss. It will take us about twenty minutes to get there with this traffic," M replied, with a particular cool-guy linguistic nuance that develops after a decade of hanging with Special Forces teams.

The Gandamak is a popular restaurant/hotel/bar frequented by foreigners in Kabul. It's always interesting to see how many of the establishment's patrons know that the place is named after the last stand of British and Indian soldiers during a retreat in 1842. During an uprising against the British, Major General Sir William Elphinstone withdrew his soldiers and support from the garrison and retreated toward Jalalabad, ninety miles to the west, during the unforgiving month of January.

As the column moved through the Hindu Kush, Afghan tribesmen mounted attack after attack after attack. Those who weren't killed from the fighting died from starvation, frostbite, and exposure from the brutal Afghan winter. Forty-five hundred British troops and 12,000 civilian workers died. The last stand of survivors fell near the Afghan village of Gandamak, the namesake of our next destination.

By the time we hit the second traffic circle, Andy was back to his steady state of calm, flipping through footwear designs on his phone. Jed and Jasmine are still less than twenty-four hours in country and are quietly taking in the sights. The amputees hobbling on wooden crutches as we pass the military hospital, daredevil cyclists riding against traffic through chaotic city circles, and bullet-holed posters of Afghanistan's national hero, Ahmad Shah Massoud, plastered on walls, cars, and billboards. "The Lion of Panjshir." It's two days until his Martyr Day, September 9. The entire nation prepares to celebrate his life, bravery, and leadership.

Before I can explain the significance of Massoud, we're in front of the Gandamack. We quickly exit the vehicle on the right and step up to the legendary and foreboding landmark. This is where the process starts to look familiar to the rest of the team. Enter through the metal gate into the containment area, bag and body check, then out through the security door into the compound.

This is my favorite part of taking newcomers to Afghanistan. Until this point, it has been a busy airport, container compound, dusty streets, and everything else you can imagine of Afghanistan. Jasmine, Jed, and Andy are about to get a treat. The feeling is somewhat like stepping through a magical closet into a new dimension of wonder.

Two taps on the security door into the compound, and it swings open to reveal a dimly lit entrance. The team enters first. I want to watch their faces after they step into the courtyard. Each one of them, in fluid motion, lift their gaze from the ground to the sight in front of them. Their eyes fully open, mouth slightly parted, all maintaining the same expression: "Was not expecting to see this in Afghanistan."

The Gandamak is symbolic of Afghanistan—centuries of art and history hidden behind compound walls. Unique architecture frames flourishing gardens, hosting conversations between cultures. Hidden historic jewels grab the eyes wherever they wander.

The Lodge is a two story building constructed of Afghan materials and British style; a single story exterior sitting room protrudes from the front of the lodge, surrounded by a stone patio that would blend seamlessly into any exterior dining area throughout Europe. Small tables for two. A few large tables to seat eight. Each of the tables candlelit, making the stucco side of The Lodge waver against the oncoming darkness of the evening. The perimeter of the patio is lined by a row of Afghan roses. The remainder of the compound is filled with a lush, green lawn. Wicker chairs sit across the lawn, surrounding low tables glowing in the candlelight.

The dining and lawn areas aren't full yet, but there are enough customers to make the low hum of conversation and laughter notable. A multitude of accents mix in the evening air—Dutch, German, French, British, Italian, and yes, the louder than most American English.

The hostess seats us at an outside table, and we let the waiter know we are waiting for two more Americans to join us. Longer hair, beards, in shape… just like every other American in country not wearing a uniform.

Sitting down at the crisp, beautifully set table, the layered dinge of travel on each of us becomes apparent. The mix of dusty dirt roads and exhaust cling to beads of sweat and have dried in place atop the base layer of international travel. We each excuse ourselves, one by one, to the bathroom to wash up. The short journey to the water closet is a history lesson about Afghanistan from the British viewpoint. Antique swords and uniforms hang on the walls. Paintings of battle scenes line the hallways. Old framed newspaper clippings are peppered throughout the building, highlighting significant moments in Afghan-British history. The entire setting makes you feel like you've traveled back in time.

After washing up and slowly strolling back to the table,

two more people have joined us: John and Eli. We've traveled halfway around the world to pick up our product from these two gentlemen. After all of the delays, Skype calls, and travel to Kabul, our hopes are high they've brought good news about delivery.

Chapter II
-Before the Beginning-

John is an anomaly. A native Pennsylvanian who spent his early twenties as a Marine engineer officer. From the stories he told, it sounded like he'd delivered lots of guns to the new Iraqi military and police and led a platoon through a variety of logistical operations across Iraq in support of the Marine Corps. It's difficult to peg him as a combat veteran by his appearance, as he bears a mixed resemblance of Ken Barbie and Jesus. His lean build represents a morning regiment of hundreds of push-ups and sit-ups.

Post departure from the military, he got involved in a toy rental business for kids. It was like the early days of Netflix where you could rent DVDs through the mail, except the product was toys. The concept is fairly simple: rent expensive toys to parents for a few weeks, then mail them back for another toy. Instead of parents dealing with disregarded mountains of battery powered Jeeps, dollhouses, and GI Joe sets, they can mail them back and get another toy to take the attention of their child until the novelty wears off. The project attracted a variety of international investors, and John was responsible for the implementation of the program.

Like many great business ideas, the idea fell apart, and John was looking for new employment. One of the investors was an Afghan family. They were impressed by his organization and work ethic. In the mid-2000s, opportunities for Afghan business with the US government was at an all-time high. The family needed someone to serve as their representative and secure business with Americans. John packed his bags and moved to Kabul.

There are laws pertaining to the procurement of clothing and equipment for service members that the United States Department of Defense must adhere to. The Berry Amendment specifically mandates that clothing for service members must be made "Fiber forward" in the United States. The DoD does this in order to maintain its supply chain in the event North America comes under attack. It would be difficult to source uniforms from China, Mexico, or any other textile center if the materials had to make it over the frontlines. The Berry Amendment is solely responsible for keeping a number of textile mills and clothing production factories in business. Essentially, it creates jobs and economic prosperity at home through billions of dollars of government-regulated procurement.

That concept is being applied in Afghanistan through the "Afghan First, Afghan Made" initiative. NATO forces spent time in Afghanistan from 2004 forward, building a 300,000+ person military and police force within the borders of Afghanistan, including the Afghan National Army and the Afghan National Police. Recruits from all over the nation pour into Kabul to receive a job, training, and a regular paycheck. Each one of those Afghans is going to need uniforms, boots, gear, and other accoutrements to be a professional soldier. They have to be procured somewhere— might as well make them in Afghanistan and create jobs along the way. Afghan companies that build boot and uniform factories will be given preferential treatment for sourcing and have access to hundreds of millions of dollars donated by the international community in an effort to secure Afghanistan from violent extremists.

John is working for a family going after those dollars. His mandate is to rehabilitate a rubbled compound into a modern boot factory capable of manufacturing hundreds of pairs of world-class combat boots daily. Over the course of two years, John and his team scoured Asia for equipment, materials, and staff who could make it happen.

We met at the Sergeant Major's Conference for the Afghan National military, an event where the senior enlisted members of the Afghan military and their international counterparts met in Kabul annually to discuss the development of the Afghan National Army. Days of meetings and demonstrations were broken up by a trade show of the newest military gear brought to you by the hungry upstarts of the American Military Industrial Complex. Tables were lined with bulletproof vests, eyewear, and optics.

My table held medical equipment consisting of rescue gear, tourniquets, and blood clotting agents. I was a young officer with long hair. Nobody was talking to me.

Across the conference center was Ken Barbie Jesus. He wore civilian attire, an Afghan scarf around his neck, and his table was bare except for a combat boot and camouflage winter jacket. Nobody was talking to him either. I'm a weird guy. He looked like a weird guy. Weird knows the value of weird. Figured I might as well introduce myself.

After a few minutes of the military equivalent of male dogs circling, we both learned how we ended up at this conference with no business. His tale of building a boot factory didn't sound terribly impressive, as John is typically quite humble, but he knew how to effectively lay the bait for a visit. "I've got the best cup of coffee in Kabul. If you're tired of drinking tea, come by the factory and have a cup," he offered.

"Deal. I'll be there tomorrow."

The following day, another salesman, Jamie, and I entered the compound through a large metal gate. Other than the security guards and John, the place appeared devoid of factory workers. The left side of the compound looked like a manufacturing facility. The white two-story industrial structure was lined with windows down the entire stretch of the second story. A large rolling door in the center. Visions of Willy Wonka rolled through my head. *That's probably where the boots come out.*

The right side of the compound looked like another industrial building for storage. Similar design, but more rolling doors for vehicle access. Immediately in front of our vehicle were forty-foot shipping containers, stacked three wide, three tall, and two deep. More materials and storage. This place was big. Much bigger than expected. John ran a legit operation.

"We're here for that coffee, John. Couldn't resist the offer."

"C'mon in. Let me show you around."

Everything past the entry door was mesmerizing. Inside that factory were hundreds of workers dressed in khaki uniforms, building gear for an army. It was dumbfounding. There was a training room to teach Afghans how to thread a sewing machine, work the pedal, and learn the basic fundamentals of becoming a cobbler. Farther down the building was the pattern room, full of Afghans tracing patterns for boots, uniforms, and tactical equipment. Past that was the big show. A huge factory space with sewing machines, an injection molding line, and thousands of pairs of boots lined across the floor. Afghans were working. Everywhere.

After four combat deployments as an officer in Special Operations, this was the first positive outcome I'd seen from all of the war. There was no blood. Nobody had a black bag over their head. And the entire facility smelled like pride. The kind of pride that came from an honest day's work; the type with the power to seep deep into the fabric of the nation and strengthen it from within.

John walked us around the floor and showed us the process from start to finish. Along the tour, he interacted with the workers by name, joked, and gave pointers for process improvements. He told tales of the factory attracting Afghan cobblers back from Pakistan, giving them the ability to work and provide for their families at home. Each person in that factory supported five to thirteen family members.

The social impact of what was going down on that floor was well beyond removing high-value targets from the battlefield. John and his team were creating the American Dream—the ability to provide the next generation a life better than they currently lived.

"John, this is amazing. Well done. What's going to happen to the factory when the war ends and the contracts run out?"

Without skipping a beat, John replied, "We're going to shut it all down. Nobody's going to want to buy anything from Afghanistan."

The feelings of amazement and inspiration immediately turned to frustration and anger.

How in the hell are we going to repeat our past mistakes in Afghanistan? Wage a protracted war, make promises of a better life, then abandon the progress, leaving a classic power vacuum that will inevitably be filled by a violent group bent on exploiting the population and rallying hate behind the message of, *See, the Americans came here, made promises, then left you with nothing but hungry bellies and destroyed homes.*

This isn't fortune telling. This is a historical inevitability.

In that moment of frustration and anger, I looked down to my half left, and there it was. Rubber. Leather. Coyote Brown. Completely badass. A combat boot sole with a flip-flop thong punch through it. It was the ugliest, coolest thing I'd ever seen.

A Combat Flip Flop. The juxtaposition of the words bounced around inside my skull. Combat: to fight.

Flip-flop: other than beach footwear, it's a political term

used to describe a person who takes a 180-degree position change on a subject.

I used to think that dropping bombs off of A-10s, flattening the earth with AC-130 gunships, and shredding flesh with airburst mortar rounds was the way to win a war. I was wrong. This was it. Jobs. Community. Family. This was how we'd win the war. Some levels of combat are obviously still required, but this option is far more effective and sustainable.

"John, you mind if I run with this?" I asked as I held up the flip-flop.

"Sure, man. Go ahead."

Afghanistan is technically a "dry" Islamic country when it comes to alcohol, but there is beer to be found, if you know a guy. Luckily, I do. With a short dog-leg detour on the way back from John's factory to the hotel, our driver stopped in front of a standard Afghan ice cream cart. Big wheels, colorful umbrella, and pictured variations of ice cream cones that were unlikely inside the cart. The driver rolled down the window and muttered a few sentences at the cart's proprietor. The ice cream man lunged his arm deep into the bottom of the cooler and produced an icy cold sixer of Heineken.

Within a few minutes, I was back in the hotel room and logging into the Wi-Fi.

www.combatflipflops.com The domain was open and

available for $2.99. I, however, had no idea how to build a website. Not knowing how to do something is about the worst reason there is to not do something.

One of the more enjoyable aspects of having served in Special Operations is the myriad personalities the career seems to attract—surfers, lawyers, professional athletes, and computer geeks alike all working through highly demanding situations together. Most members of the community share the commonality of being intelligent, hard-working, and well-versed in problem solving. My best friend in the military was Private Donald Lee. We got to know each other during mutual periods of discomfort in the field and on deployments.

Lee grew up in Boyle Heights, a notorious hispanic gang neighborhood in Los Angeles. He somehow managed to avoid all the gangs as a skate punk and was drawn to the California internet community in the late 90s. He thrived in the dot-com boom as a web designer, music producer, and video editor. Following the events of September 11, 2001, he immediately went to the recruiting office to enlist in the Army, eventually becoming an Airborne Ranger at the age of twenty-five.

During our time together in 2nd Ranger Battalion, Lee earned the nickname, "The World's Deadliest Barista." He could make a mean cup of coffee anywhere on the planet. When shit hit the fan, and it often did, I could always count on him to keep a cool head and dig in for the dirty work. Lee was notorious for questioning the mission plan with a cavalier attitude. Then, without skipping a beat, he'd make suggestions that would immediately make the plan easier, faster, and more effective. I hated it when he was right. And he often was.

He'd been out of the army for a few years now. We'd talk every few months to check in on each other and bounce business ideas back and forth. Our last one was "Café Racer." A motorcycle outfitted with an espresso machine to deliver coffee to offices. Almost as dumb as making flip-flops in Afghanistan.

It was two a.m. his time in Los Angeles. He'd be awake. After a seemingly never ending series of numbers punched into the Afghan burner phone, the familiar domestic ringtone came through the receiver. Two rings later, I heard his understandably disgruntled voice. "Who is this? And why are you calling me at two in the morning?"

"Hey, Lee. It's Griff. I'm in Afghanistan. Got an idea for you." After a few short minutes relaying the experience of what I'd seen in that factory, he understood the opportunity.

On our first deployment together, he had an experience that changed his perceptions of Afghans. Under the cover of total darkness and into two feet of snow, we stepped off the back ramp of a Chinook helicopter. Lee's platoon was in the lead, tasked with clearing a village. His job specifically was to communicate with and control the AC-130 gunship circling overhead.

He hadn't let on prior to the mission that he'd been

39

feeling ill. By the time he was in a blocking position, his fever was in the 102 range. He conducted the op in a near delirious state before passing out under a rocky overhang. A few hours later, he woke up in a puddle of melting snow and human shit. Apparently, the Afghans used that overhang to stay dry while dropping turds.

As the sun rose, it was Lee's turn to take watch. He and a fellow Ranger covered the road leading into the village. Febril. Shivering. Covered in shit. Hating life. Two young Afghan girls approached his position with cups of hot tea, flatbread, and marmalade. A gift, a simple gesture that saved him, in more ways than one.

"Yeah, man. I'm in." Lee continued without hesitation, "I'll get the website registered now."

In January of 2012, at just after two o'clock in the morning, Pacific Time, Combat Flip-Flops was born.

Pride, unbridled enthusiasm for the future, hope, and trepidation all follow birth, in business and life. Sleep deprivation, self-doubt, frustration, and inevitable feelings of failure are never far behind.

Not long after my return from Afghanistan, my wife's younger sister was getting married. For me, that meant a new member of the family in the form of a brother-in-law. The first time I met him, he showed up at a lake party with a potato cannon. After observing him spend an hour hurling spuds into Lake Chelan with the kids, I knew I liked him.

The process of making friends as an adult can sometimes be a bit awkward, even more so when you're in a merging family. A time-honored tradition known as "The Bachelor Party" often fast tracked those friendships.

Andy was almost forty and had a lifetime of experiences and friends from all over the country showing up to his party. The plan was for everybody to meet in Seattle, hop in a Suburban, drive to Spokane to pick up the last member of the crew, then party in Bozeman all weekend. The event came with two rules: no drugs and no strippers. I took those as the hard limits, meaning everything else was basically open for discussion.

After life in the Regiment, you learn to pack light for an adventure. The basic loadout for this trip consisted of a duffel bag full of guns and ammo, one change of clothes, a five pound bag of pretzels, and a thirty pack of the Pacific Northwest's Vitamin R—Rainier Beer.

We were westbound toward Spokane, Andy at the wheel. I rode shotgun, and the pastor was in the back. Flying down the 90, a heavy yet melodic pump of progressive metal poured out the open windows, all heads bobbing in unison.

"This band is filthy. Who is this?" I asked.

"Oh. It's Sunder. It's my band," Andy replied casually.

"What do you mean 'your band?'"

"I played bass in a metal band from Montana that sang songs about Montana. Matt Ranta in the back is the lead guitar on this." He pointed at another member of the party, sitting two rows back.

That was the moment Andy became my brother.

It didn't take long for the camaraderie to build. Before we knew it, we picked up the last member of the crew from the Spokane Airport. The group was complete. We reorganized the seating arrangement for the last leg into Bozeman. Somehow Andy and I got crammed into the third row seat in the back of the Suburban. Since we were going to be living together at family events for the remainder of our adult lives, we got to know each others' backgrounds. Eventually we came around to my time in the military.

I'm a fourth generation service member, West Point graduate, Army Ranger with tours in Afghanistan and Iraq. Andy was raised by a retired Navy Explosive Ordnance Disposal (EOD) technician. If there was one man I'd put up against Chuck Norris, it would be Andy's stepfather, Bob. After his early exposure, Andy wanted nothing to do with the military. We were still feeling each other out. There are plenty of preconceived notions about veterans these days.

When making the decision to tell a person about your time in service, there is equal chance to be erroneously thought of as a hero as there is to be considered a ticking PTSD bomb on the brink of detonating. In reality, the overwhelming majority of veterans fall as far away from one of those designations as the other—right in the moderate center.

In an effort to quell his concerns that his future brother-in-law could be a GWOT Walter Sobchak, I brought up the idea for a company I wanted to start. "I want to use a combat boot factory in Afghanistan to make flip-flops, sell them in the United States, keep the factory open making peaceful shit." This brought about a deliberate line of questioning from Andy.

"What kind of footwear would you make? Materials? How many people do you think it would employ? Can you support volume?" The inquiries were as abundant as the beer as evening progressed, with no drugs or strippers in sight.

The remainder of the weekend blurred into Christmas sweaters, shots fired, a bachelor party task list that should never be put into the hands of an Army Ranger, and an acquired asylum wheelchair which still sits in Andy's office today.

On Tuesday, with the residual effects of the Vitamin R still present, Andy called, "Hey, man, are you free to talk this evening?"

"Yeah, dude. I'm home making dinner. Come on by."

Andy showed up twenty minutes later with a notepad. "Hey, man, tell me more about the flip-flops you were wanting to design."

"You mean the AK's?"

"Yeah. Think you could help me sketch them out?"

"Sure, man. The product needs to tell a story. A story that would help a guy look good in front of a cute girl."

"Huh?"

"It's about the story. Americans buying products from Afghans to help end the war. What girl isn't going to find that impressive? Plus, they're just going to look sick."

43

"Let's do it."

For the next hour, we developed the number one, the AK-47. Named after the weapon of choice for low-dollar revolutionaries, it was going to have a similar color scheme, AK-casings on the straps, and it would look boss.

Andy disappeared for two days before I received another phone call. "Hey, man. I learned SketchUp and got a rendering done for the AK. Wanna see it?"

"You learned what?"

"SketchUp. It's an illustrator program. I learned it yesterday and made a drawing."

"You learned the software and made the flip?"

"Yeah, It's pretty cool. I'll be over in twenty."

And there it was—an idea, to spoken word, to drawing, to digital rendering on paper in blocky illustrated form. The AK-47. Our weapon of choice for the new revolutionaries.

Chapter III
-Social Relevance-

We started with an idea and a little bit of technology. The popularity of social media was on the rise. Facebook seemed like a logical place to post a couple of photos, gain feedback on market viability, and determine if the idea would work.

We made a few drawings, dropped them onto a free Facebook page, and shared them with friends. The caption went something like, "Hey, we're thinking about making flip-flops in a combat boot factory in Afghanistan. What do you think about these designs? What would you pay for them?"

We were only a few years out of the military. Our primary group of friends were fellow service members. Up until this point, we primarily used social media as a means to stay in touch, send dirty jokes, and lovingly harass one another. That group of experienced combat veterans saw the idea we presented and understood the potential impact it could have. They hit like, share, and commented.

"Make that shit burly."

"Why the hell are you making a Navy SEAL flip-flop?"

"I'll buy some only if you promise to chub them."

"I want you to draw a picture of a unicorn fighting a giant squid on the receipt."

Then the private messages started rolling in.

"Hey, man, I like the idea. Those people need jobs. If there's one thing we could do to stop the fighting, it would be employment."

"Great idea. How can we support?"

"I worked in the DoD business development programs. You need any help?"

The primary group of believers were seasoned hitters, quiet professionals who did what their country asked of them, fought valiantly in support of their brothers and sisters, then eventually retired into the general population. We knew some of them personally, others by reputation. Some of them were total strangers, but our mutual friends were other highly respected members of the veteran community. We looked up to all of them as warriors, heroes, and legends.

They understood the nuance and need for this mission. They'd been there, they witnessed firsthand the actions of desperate men. They'd been kept up at night with the looming frustration of giving everything you had to the wrong part of the right cause.

Others were older warriors who served in Vietnam. Men and women in their sixties started reaching out. They'd fought virtually the same war three decades prior and watched the mistakes repeated in Afghanistan. They had time and experience on their side. After the withdrawal of American forces from Vietnam, they watched commercial development change the nation in globally recognized ways. Somehow they found their way to our Facebook page and recognized the value of the product, the mission, and the story. Plus, they had disposable income and wanted to buy.

Day after day, the likes, shares, and comments kept pouring in. Regardless of age, the commonalities were undeniable: belief, hope, empathy, compassion, and a propensity for action resonated in every correspondence. Despite the facts presented to us daily and reinforced by history, they believed we could conduct ourselves differently and generate a positive outcome. There was real hope that we'd actually make a product and put people to work. A mission founded on empathy for the people living in war zones, compassion to act upon that empathy, and a general attitude of, "I dare you idiots to try and make flip-flops in Afghanistan."

The story was gaining more momentum every day, an army forming around a cause: save lives by creating jobs. Empower the mindful consumer to manufacture peace through trade.

Basically, we'd take on a bunch of risk, make products in war zones, create jobs, and teach Afghan entrepreneurs how to interact with the global market. The jobs created would provide an opportunity for steady work instead of taking fifty dollars to plant a backpack bomb or shoot the first unsuspecting whitey.

Night after night, we'd drag lines of men dressed in Afghan garb with a black, nylon bag over their head into the military detention centers. As soon as the bag was removed and the questioning started, the majority of new arrivals began the same story: "There's no jobs. What else are we supposed to do to support our family?" It doesn't take a military genius to figure out the trend.

The cost of hiring a fighter to make the US media is fairly low. If you're a marketer, the CPM metric is astoundingly low. Four hundred dollars for an AK. Ten dollars or so for ammo. Two hundred to four hundred dollars to pay a local to shoot an American. Bam…US Nightly News. "US Service Member Killed in Afghanistan." Less than $1000 to take a life and get exposure of your lethality to millions of Americans. If you're able to disconnect yourself from the emotion of it, it's fairly genius.

Put yourself in their sandals (the enemy rarely wears shoes). You hide across an international border where military forces can't attack you, and the resident government looks the other way. You have an established network of cross-border routes and carriers fueled by the opium trade. And you don't have to go through TSA to kill infidels. You have an endless supply of revenue, guns, and fighters operating from a defensible fighting position against a big, slow, predictable enemy restrained by "laws" and "rules of engagement." If you want to get your Jihad on, this is the dream—at a discount. For less than $1000, you can kill an American, fulfill your Jihad dream, protect your revenue source, and slow bleed a nation into a grave halfway around the world.

The truly sad part is that often times the one on the

controlling part of a gun or IED are typically just trying to provide for their families. Since 2001, men and women in uniform have been rolling up to villages in hurclean vehicles, making promises of prosperity that they can't keep. They attempt to work with the military leaders and economic experts on crops or schools, but it's simply a matter of time before they leave. When the armored vehicles pull away, the ever-present enemy emerges from the mountains to punish the alignment with the "infidels." Men, women, and children die. It's sad. And it happens year after year. So what does a guy with no education and a starving family do? You take the money where you can get it, feed your family as long as you can, and play the game until you're dead. That's the reality for millions of Afghans.

Here's another layer of the problem: sergeants, lieutenants, and captains are not trained in business or stability. They're trained to fight and win wars. However, they're typically on the business end of business in Afghanistan. Occasionally you'll get a Department of Commerce, USAID, or State representative wide-eyed in the field, but they have the same problem. They're really not trained in business. They're educated, but not trained.

For years, the US government surveyed the resources, conducted studies, developed training programs, invested billions of dollars into economic development—and they universally failed. They failed for two main reasons: there wasn't a customer, and even if there was a customer, they couldn't move the product affordably.

Outside of the bourgeois folks in the know, not too many

people are in the market for hand-tied wool rugs or saffron. Agricultural products such as melons, grapes, and mulberries are available in the market at a lower cost simply due to transport. Afghan products are virtually unknown to the consuming Western markets. If the customer doesn't know about your product, they're not going to buy it. If the customer isn't loyal to the brand, they're not going to buy it. If the customer believes the people who make the products are killing their service members, they aren't going to buy it. The customers required in the globally accepted supply/demand economic model simply aren't demanding the product, so there's no reason for supply. No requirement for supply means no sustainable jobs. No jobs means you take any opportunity available to feed your family. See where we're going with this?

There's a prolific line in the military and in business: "Amateurs talk tactics. Professionals talk logistics." You can make a product all day long, but if you can't get it to market, you don't have a real product. And if you can get it to market, but the cost of transport increases the delivered costs of goods sold (COGS), you'll be beat by the local competition if you don't take a beating on your margins. This is simple business mathematics. And it's the cement around the feet of Afghanistan's production economy in a sea of global competition.

It's plain geography. Afghanistan is landlocked and has few options for transporting exports. To the west, there's Iran. It would be a simple two-day drive to the port of Chabahar and a short sail across the Gulf of Aiden to enter one of the world's largest ports in Dubai. But sadly, no. Westerners and Iran don't get along very well. Something about state-sponsored terrorism and nuclear proliferation. So that route is closed.

To the east and south, there's Pakistan. Since 2001, it's been the main logistical route for the coalition effort in Afghanistan. Goods and supplies land in the ports of Karachi and are trucked across the Afghan border to major military bases. Yes, this is the same Pakistan that is providing safe harbor to the organization the coalitions fight against—but we digress. We're talking commercial efforts here.

Pakistan produces similar products and agriculture to Afghanistan. Essentially, they're the commercial competition. If you were Pakistan, what would you do to the competition? You'd make it expensive and cumbersome for them to get goods across the border and to the market— pricing out Afghan products. So they do.

To the north is Turkmenistan, Uzbekistan, and Tajikistan. There's the ability to export products via train in Turkmenistan and Uzbekistan, but that route is slow, crosses a few borders, and prices out the finished product. Plus, the terrain precludes exports out of the north. With the main agricultural and production centers of Afghanistan in the south, producers would need to truck their products through mountain passes of the Hindu Kush that separates northern and southern Afghanistan.

Interesting fact, the word, "Kush," means "killer." Invading armies would cross the Hindu Kush mountains to capture Hindu slaves. If the slaves survived the mountain passes on the army's homeland, they were considered good slaves. The terrain is so unforgiving that many did not survive, and the mountain range earned the eternal label of the "Hindu Killers." As the authors of this book know from firsthand experience, moving anything across this mountain range is a dangerous, time-consuming, and a weather-dependent adventure. Not exactly a route that supports viable commercial development.

North, south, east, and west, ground routes are simply fucked. Afghanistan is surrounded by nations funding terrorism, filled with commercial competition, and restricted by terrain. Amateurs talk tactics, professionals talk logistics. We've been talking tactics for years, not fully realizing the logistical limitations preventing commercial development within the borders of Afghanistan.

Where were we? Oh yes, the Facebook.

As social media interest continued to build, we started talking logistics.

How much is this going to cost to actually make footwear?

How many will we need to sell in order to get an initial run going?

How the fuck do you make flip-flops?

The flips looked good on paper, but you couldn't wear that shit. We had to find somebody who actually knew how to make footwear. Through some mutual friends, I had a contact at a major shoe manufacturer named Paul Litchfield. One of Lee's first jobs out of the military was web design and marketing for a footwear retailer in Los Angeles. As a result, he knew people who were in the business of making private footwear. These were two good sources to help make this a reality. We rallied our respective networks to advance the mission.

Paul is five-feet-eight-inches of wiry Boston boxer. It's tough to tell by his energy that he's somewhere in his fifties. The man is a specimen of physical care and hard work. He talks fast, loves making shoes, boxing, and making his own lumber at his property in Connecticut. He is also the inventor of the Reebok Pump, held the position of VP of Product Development at Reebok, and knows just about everything there is to know about shoes, down to the molecular level. Talking to him is a mix of chemistry, swearing, factory management, tales of his kids, and a healthy dose of shit-talking. Paul is a legend.

"Paul, I was thinking about starting a footwear company." And I started in with the tale.

"Griff. That's a great idea. Crazy. But still a great idea. How can I help?"

And like that, we had a footwear legend onboard. We showed him the renderings, he made suggestions on the materials, estimated product costs, and gave thoughts on the most important detail—how many to make in the first run. You can make anything you want. It's just a matter of how much you want to pay for it. With 35 years of footwear production experience, he gave an estimate.

"Two thousand. Given the sizing and style count, you're going to need to make about 2,000 pairs of flip-flops to make it worthwhile in production and not take a beating on material costs."

Two thousand pairs didn't seem like an overwhelming number. At a retail price of around $70, we would need to buy them for roughly $25 to make the margins work. That would be $50,000 for production, but if we sold them for $70 a pair, there would be a profit potential of $90,000, assuming everything went smoothly.

So all we had to do was convince 2,000 people that it would be a good thing to make flip-flops in Afghanistan? Hold my beer.

Andy called Lee. "Lee. Can you get a hold of your guys at the footwear place and see if they'll be able to do a run of 2,000 pairs."

"Yeah, man. Sure. I'll give them a call tomorrow."

Within a week, there was a meeting set in Los Angeles with the suppliers. Andy and I flew down to LA.

Los Angeles, the prominent heartbeat of yesterday's American dream, asphyxiated by noxious effluviums of ego and tail pipe alike, complete with fetid arterial infarction.

Lee picked us up and drove through an hour's worth of the bleeding gray cesspool's whiplash inducing stop-and-go traffic before we arrived at the headquarters of a local footwear distributor.

The process seemed straight forward. We handed them drawings, specified colors and materials, and gave them a spreadsheet of the sizing curves by style. They said they'd get back to us with pricing and a timeline for tooling development, prototypes, and raw material costs. Could it really be that easy? Could we really be on the way to taking an idea from spoken word, to paper, to graphic design, to a real item?

Afghanistan doesn't have tooling manufacturers, leather tanneries, or rubber trees. It's impossible to make conventional footwear from the raw materials within the borders of Afghanistan. So you have to buy materials from China, Pakistan, or Vietnam and export them to Afghanistan for final assembly. Expensive? Yes. Worth it? TBD.

Within a few weeks, the contract for services were in the company inbox. Twenty five hundred dollars to make the prototypes for photo sampling. That was a lot smaller of a risk than the full $50,000 production run. Maybe we could take photo samples and presell them? We'll simply tell people that they have to wait until there's enough volume to make the production run. If they don't sell, we only ate $2,500.

At the time, $2,500 to make flip-flops in Afghanistan wasn't exactly in the family budget. None of us were swimming in dough, so we did what most entrepreneurs do—we sold some of our belongings. To this day, the idea that the seed money for this company was provided by the sale of a chopper and two long guns bought with deployment dollars provides me with a deep sense of satisfaction.

A few months later, a moderately sized box showed up on the back porch via DHL. It was from China and contained nine pairs of flip flops. There were three styles put forward by three different factories with variations on each style. There it was. The effort. We went from idea, to spoken word, to digital rendering, to physical form. The mission manifested.

Over the next two days, Andy poured over each detail of the nine pairs. He's such a dork, and if you wear our footwear, you can thank him for it. With his cell phone, and a construction app that enabled comments on photo images of a project, he outlined the pros and cons of each pair. By the second day, Andy assembled a brief for the team that outlined the next evolution of Combat Flip Flops—the production samples.

Shape, curve, materials, colors, heat stamps, logo locations, EVA durometer, blah blah blah. Andy sourced feedback from Lee and me, then sent off the email for the production prototypes. It all seemed to progress with ease and what felt like a gravitational pull. What we were doing felt right. It felt good.

We received three styles: The AK-47's, The Poseidons, and The Tuck Tucks. All size 9. Andy borrowed a nice DSLR camera and took a few candid shots on his kitchen counter. Within twelve hours of arriving, we took photos, posted them on our Facebook page, and emailed a few tactical and military bloggers. Idea, to spoken word, to drawing, to digital rendering, to physical form, and offered to the wolves.

The response was overwhelmingly positive, but the response from Soldiersystems.net was the game changer.

Soldier Systems Daily is a running blog of new products and programs for the military community. Guns, camo, body armor, and now…Combat Flip Flops. They get hundreds of thousands of unique monthly views, and lots of eyeballs saw the images and product descriptions. The messages started hitting the inbox faster than we could respond.

"When are these going to be available? Do you make them in a size fifteen? Are they wide or narrow?"

It was a Cheshire-Cat-smile moment. We were going to sell 2,000 pairs of flip-flops and get that factory working. The mission was manifesting itself in front of us.

It was the fall of 2011. We felt pressure to be ready for spring 2012 flip-flop season. If we got that many positive responses from one military blog, then we'd just have to meet a bunch of military bloggers to generate the volume to make it happen. Show them the newest, coolest flip-flops on the planet, made by veterans, in a war zone. They'd dig it. But where would we meet them?

If you're going to sell anything to the tactical or outdoor industries, you attend the SHOT Show and Outdoor Retailer Show, respectively. If you're unfamiliar, SHOT Show is just about the most testosterone-fueled event you can image. Military, law enforcement, and outdoor enthusiasts descend upon Las Vegas to walk acres of convention floor full of machine guns, body armor, guns, 4x4s, guns, knives, and more guns.

This bustling hive of tactical activity meant one important thing for our mission: media. Countless writers who already had the audience of our desired demographic descended upon the spectacle every year to cover everything from new camo patterns to which military T-shirt company threw the best party.

SHOT Show is always held in Las Vegas in January. That was our backstop, and it was quickly approaching. We had to figure out the target bloggers, make contact, get their shoe sizes, and make appointments to meet them in Sin City in less than ninety days.

The Wookie was on it.

The week before SHOT Show, Andy's living room was covered in flip-flops— 200 pairs of them. We had to sell a boat and a few more guns to make it happen, but there they were. Two hundred weapons for change ready to be deployed into the world. They were to be issued to bloggers and left to the mercy of the internet.

Getting a booth at SHOT Show is ridiculously expensive. Ten thousand dollars for a ten foot by ten foot booth in the basement. Besides being outside the window to register for a booth, we didn't have the money. We needed to get creative.

We didn't even have passes to get in. I had several friends who I could have borrowed them from, but the idea of launching the company out of a duffel bag with a borrowed name tag didn't seem fitting for the mission. There had to be a better solution.

"Andy, there's a bar right at the corner of the convention center, with the Venetian, the Palazzo, and restaurants. It's called the Public House. I think they open at eleven. We could post up there and have the bloggers meet us."

"So we're gonna show them the footwear, give them beer, and ask them to write about the company in a bar?"

"Basically."

"Yeah, let's do that. Is the website ready to take orders?"

"What website?"

"The one to take the pre-orders. We should call Lee."

In the history of the mission, the following story has been debated from two viewpoints. Since I'm the one writing this book, you'll get mine. Sorry, Lee.

"What the fuck do you mean I have to build a website to take orders in a week?" Lee objected in his affectionately cantankerous way.

"Yeah, man. We're headed to SHOT Show next week. There's going to be lots of web traffic. We should start taking money if we're going to make this thing happen."

"Fuck you." I knew from the soft way he let the first syllable play out that he wasn't mad. He's an artist with expletives, capable of delivering complex myriad human emotions with that one single F-word. If you're not familiar with the unique lexicon of the profane, the translation for this "fuck you" was, *I'm going to do this, but you could have given me more time.*

"Love you too, bro."

The doors to the Public House opened properly at eleven a.m. The place was hip, had a good view of the trade show intersection, and the lounge booths had tables big enough to hold drinks and three pairs of flip-flops. It was perfect.

Andy pulled our server aside. "Hey, if we give you $100 now and $100 more on top of the standard tip, can we occupy one of these booths for the day?"

"If you're going to be buying drinks and food, stay as long as you like. If the manager asks you to leave, I can't do anything about that. Cool?"

Nods of agreement and an exchange of cash, and just like that we had the first Combat Flip Flops SHOT Show booth. Kind of.

For the next few hours, industry friends and bloggers poured through, took photos, posted to social media, and sent the idea out to the firearms world. All while drinking a beer. Not a bad way to make a living.

Then the phone and email started blowing up. People were seeing the posts, and the messages and sales poured in. They started with a slow trickle, then progressively picked up momentum.

"Hey, Andy. Guess what?"

"What?"

"We're selling flip-flops."

It was happening. Idea, to word, to sketching, to digital rendering, to sample, to broadcast, to legitimate sales. The feeling was unreal. People read about the mission, thought it was a good idea, and trusted us with their money to get it done. The reality hadn't yet set in on what we were about to do.

Compulsively, I checked the inbox. The orders continued to pour in. Then a different subject line interrupted the sales notifications.

Subject: When are these available?

The email was pretty simple. It was a dealer in Australia

who wanted to buy some.

Reply:

> Hi. We're at SHOT Show in Vegas making initial sales. We'll have more information about delivery timelines in the next few weeks.

> Send.

Immediate reply:

> : I'm at SHOT Show too. Want to meet?

> : Where are you now?

> : Palazzo Circle Bar.

The Public House and Palazzo Circle Bar are roughly 200 yards apart.

> : We'll meet you there.

"Andy, let's settle the tab and go meet a dealer."

With a quick swipe of the card, we were on our way. A few minutes later, we stepped up to the Circle Bar. The place was crammed full of muscle-bound, bearded, tattooed gun lovers laughing and giving each other shit. Cops, operators, and gun manufacturers getting their pre-game on before dinner. The energy was high, and the vibe was good.

Graham was sitting at a table toward the back. He looked every bit the part of an Australian businessman: cool haircut, nice button-down, sport coat. Professional. He made an excellent first impression. Andy and I, on the other hand, were a little disheveled after our long day drinking beers at the Public House.

Graham didn't mince words. "I'd like to sell your products in Australia."

"That's cool. How many stores do you have?"

"No. I want the whole country of Australia. I'll be a distributor."

"Yeah? Can you handle 2,000 units? If you can, you can have the rights to Australia."

"Shouldn't be a problem."

The reality hit like a lucky slot machine. We were going to make this thing happen. It was fucking working. Holy shit. Idea, to word, to sketching, to rendering, to prototype, to the masses, and now…production.

"Can you wire us a fifty percent deposit? We'll have the order to you by Fall."

"Deal. Let's get the paperwork sorted after SHOT. Want a beer, mate?" There's something about an Australian accent that makes the offer of a beer even more enticing. Add to that, Graham was excited about the new partnership. We were excited about the partnership. We drank the beer. The beer was delicious. Life was delicious.

We still had a few more bloggers to run down. The phone's persistent vibrating with sales notifications enabled us to shake hands, smile, and carry on with sales activities. I had to call Lee and let him know what was going on.

"Lee."

"Yeah."

"We just sold 2,000 pairs of flip-flops to an Australian distributor. He's gonna wire us a deposit."

"What?"

"Yeah, man. We have enough orders to start the run. This is happening."

"The website is on fire right now. I bet we sell another thousand by the end of the week."

"Love you, bro. Gotta go."

"Fuck You." This time he said it in a way that conveyed, *I should have driven my ass to Vegas to be a part of this. Have fun.*

Andy's gears were turning. On the walk back to the hotel room, he was already trying to put the production calendar together in his head. Two months to make materials. One month in shipment to Afghanistan. A month in production. A month to ship to the US. Five months from today.

"Griff, if all things line up, we could hit a June delivery."

"Seems to be working so far. I'll tell people June. Let's get a hold of John for a meeting next week."

With a few thumb swipes and rapid tapping on the iPhone, I sent an email to John in Kabul. It was time to make some flip-flops.

Within a few hours, John replied.

> I'm at SHOT Show in Vegas. Let's talk about it when the show's over.

You can't make this shit up. The mission had taken on an energy all its own, and it was gravitational. It was impossible to get away from the pull.

The next morning we woke up feeling giddy. Yes, giddy. We'd sold neary 3,000 pairs of flip-flops in a single day. By noon, we were back at the official Combat Flip Flops SHOT Show booth in the Public House. This job didn't suck to begin with and seemed to be getting better by the hour. Now we were about to have a beer with John and his business partner, Eli, about making the flip-flops.

We'd been sitting for a few minutes when John and Eli walked in. Every interaction I'd ever had with John reaffirmed my belief he's the direct descendant of the most interesting man alive. The dude simply has style. Eli was his muscle, physically and metaphorically, slightly shorter than John, but stacked twice as wide. If it weren't for his smile, he'd be seriously intimidating. They served together in the Marine Corps in Iraq. John hired Eli to help with the footwear factory. The pair sat down with the competence and skepticism earned from two years manufacturing footwear in Afghanistan.

"Who would have thought it would work, huh, John?" I joked as we shook hands

"No kidding."

For the next few minutes, we discussed the state of the orders and the need for production. There was bad news. The factory lost its military boot contract. They had to close the doors. Everybody had to go home after the last production runs were delivered in a few months. The exact thing we were trying to prevent happened right undeath our feet. With thousands of orders and a handshake deal for an Australian distributor, this was a moment we could have used Lee's mastery of the profane.

I asked John, "Is there anything we can do?"

"Looking at the timeline, we could likely get your order after the last boots are produced. One run, then done."

"Let's do it."

"Yeah, but there's something else."

"What?"

"The shipping route to Afghanistan through Pakistan is closed."

Pakistan closed the border crossing points for coalition materials due to a cross-border engagement with dangerous people standing in Afghanistan. The Pakistanis lost and got kind of pissed about it and decided to shut down the entire logistical chain for the Afghan war effort. Convoys were stacked up for miles at the border. People were even setting some of the trucks on fire. It wasn't a good situation for anyone.

"We'll have to truck the materials through the -stans—or airlift. It's either going to be slow or expensive."

"Can you do it?"

"Yeah. We can do it."

Andy and Eli were kindred spirits. The production guys. Or as the they liked to say, "Keep the promises made by the sales guys." They immediately began planning details over tall, frothy beverages. Life was still delicious.

The following months flew by. Sales slowed but

continued to trickle in. By the time the material production cutoff arrived, we had sold 4,000 pairs. There was at least 4,000 people in the world who thought making flip-flops in a combat boot factory was a good idea. To put it in comparison, the student body of West Point is roughly 4,000 people.

We had assembled a brigade of customers. A small army of revolutionaries. Badass humans who felt compelled to do something positive. Instead of bitching about the problems in Afghanistan, they took action, and it wasn't difficult for them to do. Less than two minutes on Combatflipflops.com and a few dollars and they were putting people to work in a combat boot factory.

Often times, all that's necessary to implement positive change is the belief that situations can improve—that and a little patience.

Chapter IV
-I Still Can't Think of Anything-

"Flashback humor."
~ T. Durden

September 2012, three years after that late night phone call to Lee, Andy, Jed, Jasmine and I sit across the candlelit table from John and Eli at the Gandamack discussing the recent challenges in Afghanistan that affected our fledgling business.

In late 2011, President Obama announced the end of US involvement in Afghanistan by the end of 2014. Procurement contract management for the Afghan military was transferred from NATO control to Afghan control. They needed to figure out how to source materials for their own Army without Big Brother looking over their shoulder. This switch lead to an assessment of the cost of buying Afghan-made products versus importing gear. Chinese gear was less expensive. With the focus on saving dollars, the "Afghan First. Afghan Made" contracts were canceled in order to spend money on less expensive military equipment. To the cost of hundreds of Afghan jobs, John had to close his doors.

John is in a tough spot. He'd agreed to make our first run

of flip-flops at SHOT, but he's being met with these constant uncontrollable challenges. Before finishing our meal, we make the final arrangements for product pickup. The link up will be at ten o'clock in the morning the following day at a compound north of Jalalabad Road.

At the end of the dinner, we confirm phone numbers, directions, and timing for pickup. The transition out of gardens and into the streets of Kabul is more shocking than the entrance. The feeling of relaxation created by a few beers and candlelight are immediately crushed with the first step out of the Gandamack. It's dark. The streets are barely lit and smell of burning garbage and open sewer.

M flashes his headlights from across the street, and all four of us quickly cross traffic to jump into the Corolla. We are a well-oiled machine at this point. Everybody enters through the same car door, place bags in the same spot, and load up just like a Ranger fire team. There isn't any waste or hesitation. We all move with speed and purpose. As we make the drive back to the sleeping container compound, Afghanistan looks dark and familiar. This is how I remember it. Quiet. The tranquility of speed through desolate city streets. Excitement building for the objective. I feel it again. Alive.

Today is the day. The realization of a dream that's been shrouded in hard work. Andy pours over spreadsheets for order counts. Jed triple checks all of his camera equipment, microphones, and accessories. Jasmine follows Jed's lead. Everything has to be right. We are only going to get this moment once. M calls from the gate. It's time to go.

The drive is roughly a mile, as the crow flies. We head north to Jalalabad Road, turn right, and within a quarter mile, turn left across traffic to the manufacturing compounds on the north side of the street. Compound by compound, the pothole sizes increase in magnitude. Afghan navigation is a miracle. Most directions go something like this:

"Orange compound across from the red tower."

"Yellow building to the left of the bakery"

You get the point. M zigs and zags the vehicle through a dirt road deserving of a Baja 1000 truck. We jam north on the final leg. I'd been here a few years before. A unique structure jogs my memory.

On the left side of the road appears to be a giant garbage dump. Bottles, cans, plastic bags, wrappers, everything discarded in a huge pile. When you look more closely, it becomes apparent the pile is quite purposeful. A smoking chimney extends a few feet in front of the pitch of the roof. There are paths cut into a steep face of the pile. Then you see the door. It's a house—made entirely of garbage

The site makes apparent just how poor Afghans are. In order to live close enough to a city to have a job and provide, a man was willing to collect garbage from which to build a home. By my recollection, he's been living in that home for at least six years.

This house exists less that two miles from lush embassy

gardens, banks, government buildings, and people spending hundreds of billions annually to fight an idea—violent extremism. Perhaps if more time was spent outside of the walls, understanding what contributes to the violence there'd be less of it. But instead of running projects to say, build affordable homes and schools, billions are spent on armored vehicles, armed drones, and troop surges. You know what they say: "If there was no profit in war, there wouldn't be any war."

We are here to change that. Provide a small example of what's possible with commercial efforts, to provide jobs and fight poverty. M's Corolla is 300 yards and closing on the location of our precious cargo—the first run of Combat Flip Flops.

The orange gate in the middle of the cement wall looks freshly painted. M honks. A few seconds later, an Afghan holding an AK snoops his head out of the window of the guard tower to the upper right of the gate and yells down to somebody inside. A rectangular viewing window slides open at head height in the front of the gate. A squinting pair of dark brown eyes peer through the opening, reviewing the car and passengers. M waves at him. The viewing window snaps shut. It feels like we're in the *Wizard of Oz, standing* at the end of the yellow brick road wondering if the cantankerous munchkin is going to let us in.

The gate slowly opens to the left, revealing a center drive down the middle of the compound. There's a tall tower at the end of the compound and storage buildings down the left and right side. It looks clean, but empty. M pulls in, and the gate immediately closes behind the car. An older man in Afghan garb approaches from the left.

The team and M immediately exit the vehicles. M approaches the older man and begins conversing. The guards from the tower and the gate join in the conversation. While they are getting sorted, Jed unpacks his camera gear in anticipation of capturing the moment of delivery. Jasmine has the camera pressed to her face. The shutter is clicking with authority. Andy and I are nervous and excited; it's an opportune time to light a rare cigarette. A large, white, guard dog comes trotting around the corner and sniffs us out.

After a few minutes, M lets us know that John and Eli are busy, and they are to show us where the product is located. The two guards walk fifty yards to the warehouse on the right and start pushing on the large sliding door. Andy and I are a few steps behind, Jasmine and Jed in tow with cameras rolling.

Solid walls extend ten feet up with a line of large windows running down the perimeter of the building to let in light and provide ventilation. As the doors slide open, the sun's rays from the east hit the windows and create partitioned streaks of light through the dusty interior of the otherwise unlit warehouse. A single, dominant dust-filled light beam lands perfectly on a huge pile of poly-bagged flip-flops on pallets, like the pot of gold at the end of an arduous rainbow. Eureka!

The main export of Afghanistan is opium. The stuff grows everywhere, fuels the global heroin trade, and funds insurgent warfare. We want our product to be the main export of Afghanistan, so we made the packaging for our footwear burlap opium sacks with big poppies screen printed on them. We now gaze at thousands of burlap opium bags stuffed with Combat Flip Flops.

Jubilant high fives and hugs of relief slowly cease as we collectively realize that M's Corolla isn't anywhere near big enough to move these flips, even in multiple trips. We need something bigger. M steps outside to the compound courtyard and starts calling friends. A few minutes later, he steps back in to let us know a truck will arrive in an hour. That means we have work to do. We grab the duffel bags from the trunk of the Corolla and start filling them with opium bags of flip-flops. My attention is drawn to the corner of the warehouse just long enough to notice the white guard dog chewing on a dead rat.

This is Afghanistan. Beauty. Inspiration. Life. Dust. Work. Hunger. Death.

It takes roughly forty-five minutes to get the bags sorted by the models: The AK-47s, Tuck Tucks and The Poseidons. The AK-47 is meant to resemble an AK-47 rifle, a reliable weapon responsible for so much violence, empowerment, and change. Brown, tan, and leather upper the same color as an AK sling. It even has cast AK-47 casings on the upper straps. The Tuck Tucks are meant to resemble the colorful three-wheeled taxis in Afghanistan. Quilted red suede deck, lime green EVA cushioning, and blue patent leather upper with a chrome poppy ornament centered on the EVA. The Poseidon is blue and tan with a Navy SEAL stamp on the deck and a wave pattern on the strap. Three models, sorted into bags and ready to get on the truck.

We finish fifteen minutes early to find Jed and Jasmine are nowhere in sight. Exiting the warehouse building into the center alley of the compound, we can see Jed shooting into an opening between the warehouse building and the guard shack opposite us.

We turn the corner to find Jasmine awkwardly holding an AK-47 on top of a pile of bricks. A few short jokes are exchanged with Jasmine before we hear the honk from the bongo truck outside the large orange gate. Our ride is here.

The blue Isuzu Cabover Truck with large yellow advertising letters painted down the side rolls into the compound. The Afghan man riding shotgun hops out and speaks with M. After exchanging a few words and hand-and-arm signals, "Shotgun" directs the truck to stop in front of the open warehouse door in front of the pile of duffel bags and opium sacks. With help, the driver backs up to the pile, and the entire group begins the fire brigade chain, moving flip-flops into the bed. Within a few minutes, the entire floor of the truck is three layers deep of duffel bags and flip-flops. Andy stands atop the pile in admiration. The truck needs to turn around, so Andy sits down on the pile of flip-flops as the Isuzu does what looks like a fifteen-point turn in the lane between the warehouses before pulling forward to the gate.

I joke with Andy, "You going to ride on those back to the compound?"

"Yes. Yes, I am."

Turning to M, I ask, "Can you follow us with Jasmine in the car?"

"Sure, boss."

"What?" Jasmine questions.

Jed chimes in, "I'm riding along too," in his Kentucky accent.

"Jasmine, can you ride with M back to the compound? Andy, Jed, and I are going to ride the flip-flops back. Can you shoot images from the car?" Jasmine is likely a little nervous about being without us, but given a task and proximity to the rest of the pack, she seems to calm down and make ready with the camera.

Handshakes and hugs all the way around to our Afghan hosts, and it's time to go. Jasmine and M pull behind our flip-flop chariot. Jed hops to the front of the bed and leans against the cab to brace his body and hold the camera steady. Andy sits mid-truck. I hop in beside him. Shotgun likely doesn't want people to throw shit at white guys in the back of his truck, so he jumps in with us. A merry group of four ready to ride triumphantly down the streets of Kabul on a pile of what appears to be 3,000 pounds of opium. When you say it out loud, it sounds a bit crazy.

The gate opens, and we slowly roll out onto the potholed dirt road. Although the truck is bigger than M's Corolla, the potholes seem to have the same effect on the passengers. All four of us sway back and forth on the flip-flops, giggling like farm kids whose parents let them ride in the back of the truck on the back roads.

The sound of techno music invades the scene. Not any techno music. It's some crazy mix of traditional Middle Eastern music and techno. And it sounds amazing, somehow perfectly echoing the excitement of our adventure through Kabul.

We turn to see a dark blue "jingle truck" heading the opposite direction down the dirt road. In the cab sits four Afghan men in their late teens, crammed into three seats. The road is too small for both trucks to fit. They pull to their right, as do we, and the slow creep begins. Both trucks narrowly fit on the road while not scratching each other's paint. At one mile per hour, their techno blares. They are smiling, dancing, and laughing like American teenagers listening to good tunes. From our perch atop the flip-flops, we begin to dance as well. As they pull beside the bed of the truck, the two groups make eye contact, and the Afghans stop and stare in amazement at the highly uncommon sight of three white guys on a pile of opium bags, grooving to their beats.

"Yeah!" Andy yells at the top of his lungs, smiling and continuing to dance.

The entire group in the jingle truck immediately return the smile, cheer, and restart their groove. The universe smiles upon us. It's a reminder that the world is a mirror. How many times have those young men driven past a group of Westerners and received the *stink eye*? What was their response?

The world is a mirror of our thoughts, words, and actions. If we put fear, anger, hate, loathing, jealousy, and lust into the world, that's what we'll receive in return. If we open our hearts and change our minds, the world will provide. It will provide in a way we've never seen before. A way we can't imagine. A way described by our religious teachers. A way we all yearn for in the hopeful corners of our hearts. "The" way.

When enough of us learn this lesson, the path will be laid in front of us all. The journey there is perilous. It's wrought with pain. It's a war. It's necessary.

You're on the path now, ascending.

Chapter V
-Packing Boxes-

I wonder if Andy's up? I hate jet lag. Three hours until the sun's up. Dammit. Can't sleep. I'm going to go stare at some flip-flops in opium bags.

It takes a few seconds of fumbling around in the dark inside the container, but eventually I find the light switch. The fluorescent bulbs pop as they warm up the dry Afghan evening air. It's sometime between late night and early morning, the hour entrepreneurs go to work. We need to figure out how to get all of the footwear home, but that will have to wait until daylight. Right now, I just want to stare at flip-flops.

There seems to be a uniform trait in most men. When we accomplish a goal, acquire a shiny state-of-the-art toy, or create something new for the universe to hold, we stare, perhaps retracing the hazardous steps down arduous roads, over formidable hurdles to arrive at the object of our desires. Or maybe this is a moment to connect with the divine human purpose to create. Seering to memory the result of quite, fervent resolve. Alone in that hour between day and night, I stand motionless in the most intriguing place on Earth, under the flicker of neon light, staring at a mountain that was once an idea.

The phone shows four a.m.

It isn't long before the door swings open behind me. It's Andy.

"Couldn't sleep either, huh, Andy?"

"Nope."

"What do you want to do?"

"Let's inventory everything and get it ready for shipment."

We start with the AKs. Andy grabs one of the bundles, puts it on the desk, grabs his knife, and opens the first bag. Within seconds of pulling the first flip-flop out of the bag, his demeanor changes.

"What's up?"

"Does this leather look right to you?"

"Looks a little different than the sample material, but it's a first run. Why?"

"It doesn't look right. The shape looks funny too. This isn't how we spec'd construction."

"Well, let's open a few more."

For the next hour, each opened bundle delivers more bad news. The leather wave on the Poseidon strap is adhered incorrectly, and the material is already peeling off. The chrome poppy hood ornament on Tuck Tucks is bubbling. Small bits of chrome are already inside the bag, and rust is starting to form. It is wrong. All of it.

We stand there—staring. Staring at thousands of pairs of flip-flops that people purchased nine months prior. They paid $70 for a badass pair of flip-flops, and then waited in anticipation for months for the team to bring them home. And now we can't. If we ship the flip-flops, it will only reaffirm that substandard goods come from Afghanistan. It will destroy any hopes for the mission moving forward. The reviews will suck. People will be pissed. The success of the mission will only be triumphed by the size of the failure.

"Griff, we need to call John, like now, and find out what the fuck happened."

"On it."

It doesn't take long before we've relayed the information to John, sent photos via email, and discovered the issue. None of us had been paying attention. We could point fingers, but we were all so busy trying to get the materials to the factory before it closed that nobody inspected the materials from the Chinese manufacturer. That miss resulted in a large pile of beautifully assembled Combat Flip Flops, made out of shitty material.

"I'll make it right." John says. "But I can't make another run."

We step outside into the early morning twilight of Kabul. Andy lights the first cigarette. I'm right behind him. We sit there. Staring. Smoking.

What are we going to do? Who are we going to call? How are we going to break this to Lee? What are the wives going to say? What are we going to tell the customers? How are we going to get the money back?

Tears roll out of both of us. Months of hard work and dreaming are lost to the perils of our situation. Lee is the first call. In typical Lee fashion, his initial shock turns immediately into steps of action.

"What are we going to do, Griff?"

"I don't know. I think the best thing we can do is tell the truth. Can you get an email out to the customers?"

"What are we going to say?"

"We'll just tell them what happened, send some pictures, and ask for some time to get it figured out. If they want a refund, let's start issuing them until we run out of cash."

"Really?"

"Got any other suggestions?"

Jed and Jasmine are awake now. They sit down at the courtyard table in the open seats next to Andy and me, smoking. "What's with the sad faces?" Jed asks.

Andy relays the news. If it weren't for the disastrous morning, the open mouth gazes from Jed and Jasmine may have been entertaining. Jed is a successful entrepreneur and photographer. He immediately understands the math behind the current situation. Jasmine begins a rapid-fire series of questions about the issue, sans solutions. Now all four of us sit there, staring.

After a few minutes, Andy stands up slowly. "I have to call Kristy. Tell her what happened."

"I'm going to call Michele."

The call home is tough. I'm standing halfway around the world from my family, relaying the bad news. The idea that turned into a business and sucked up countless hours away from the family and all the spare cash is dead. We've failed. She takes it well. Sad, but well. Then she asks the same question everyone else has asked, "What are you going to do?"

"I don't know. Our plane doesn't leave for a few days. We're going to need some time to figure it out."

"Love you."

"Love you too. I'll call you tomorrow."

Within a few hours, all of the relevant players know the situation. Andy and I snap a few photos of the footwear, craft a message, and send it to Lee for distribution to the customers.

What do you do when you're going through hell? You keep going.

Prior to arriving in Kabul, we knew John's factory would be closing. We have to find a backup factory. From what we know of the Afghan First, Afghan Made program, there are three factories in town making boots. We'd emailed with one a few months prior and let them know what we were doing. They wanted to help. Andy organized material samples and specification packages for the factory and sent them ahead of our arrival. We scheduled an appointment to meet them this afternoon. We have to put our big boy pants back on and do business.

There's a rumor of another factory farther down Jalalabad Road, across from the Kabul Military Training Center. It just reopened after a massive fire. We haven't been in contact with them, but we know a few people who can put us in touch.

While the team organizes their gear for the day, I call my contact at the Department of Commerce in Kabul. Walt is a seasoned businessman who thoroughly enjoys international work. Over the years, he held a variety of jobs that eventually landed him as the subject matter expert for the United States, developing trade and commerce in

Afghanistan. He exudes optimism and figure-it-outness. Walt is a professional problem solver.

"Give me a day or two. I'll see what I can do." Walt pauses for a brief moment before adding, "I'll call you back if I find anything."

M is waiting at the gate, on time. The four of us pile into the Corolla for the short drive down Jalalabad Road to a boot factory that closed months prior. One hundred yards to the big, green gas station, turn right, and enter Kabul's morning traffic. Less than a mile down the road, we turn left across traffic and immediately stop in front of a large compound. When I say large, I mean huge. It's the biggest factory-looking compound on the block. Massive walls, guard towers, and industrial-sized buildings big enough to park commercial airliners.

"This it?" I ask M.

"This is it, boss."

The gate opens and we roll in. The facility is immense—way bigger than John's boot factory. The family contact meets us outside the gate. He's a thin Afghan man dressed in business shoes, dress slacks, and a fashionable button-down shirt. He is kind, yet professional, and takes an immediately liking to Jasmine.

The building adjacent to the parking area is an office space. We're escorted to a meeting room fashioned in traditional Afghan decor, complete with cups of tea waiting and bowls of sugar-coated almonds on the tables. We sit, build relationships, talk family, discuss the mission—the desire to make footwear in Afghanistan—the failed run, and options to get product delivered by spring. Despite the loss we sustained hours before, we begin to feel hope again.

After an hour, the meeting room door opens, and a man informs the boss that the workers are on the factory floor making the prototypes. It's time to take the tour and witness their manufacturing capabilities. We exit the headquarters building and walk to another large building, 150 yards across the courtyard.

As we pass through the entrance, it takes a few seconds for our eyes to adjust and see the scale of their production. Hundreds of sewing machines are lined up in perfect factory uniformity. The machines are covered in plastic, and the plastic is covered in dust, an image that told an all too common, yet heartbreaking story. Months before, hundreds of workers ran those machines. The feeling of lost hope is palpable in the cavernous room.

Half a dozen Afghans huddle around a few tables near the door. The table is covered in flip-flop leather, EVA, and fabric. They discuss, pour over the drawings, and begin collecting tools before uncovering a few machines and flipping switches. It's time to make some flip-flops.

Andy is enthralled by the entire process. Layers of rubber are coated with primer then left to sit. Leather decks mate with the EVA mid-layer and run through the sewing machine. Thongs punch through the decks and stretch across the plastic foot forms to create the shape. Parts are reglued again, and then pressed together and squeezed in a press to ensure the entire mating surface of the materials is bonded. A rough flip is pulled from the press. Andy observes intently as the edges are meticulously run across a sander to even the sandwiched layer of material.

"Griff, look at how they—"

BOOM!

Andy's observation is interrupted violently by the unmistakable sound of high explosives. A bomb has just gone off. The sound, the vibration, feels common, familiar. I forget, however, that it is the rest of the team's first time in a war zone. Andy, Jed, and Jasmine look around with concern.

"What was that?" Jasmine asks.

I make an effort to quell her mild unease. "Sounded like a bomb. Not too close though. We're good. Let's find out what's going on and see if it's safe to move around town."

A few short minutes later, notifications of the attack make it to us. A bomb exploded near the diplomatic corridor. A vending booth frequented by expats and soldiers was blown up. Likely a suicide bomber.

We're making flip flops and people are dying. Perspective.

"Do you think anybody is going to report the attack?" Jasmine asks with a wild look in her eye.

"I'm sure somebody will," I respond.

"I want to go."

"What?"

"I want to see it. If we're going to tell this story, we need to capture this."

"Jed, your thoughts?"

"Yeah. I'll go."

A few short minutes later, Jed and Jasmine load into M's Corolla. A newfound seriousness grabs the musculature of each of their faces. Perhaps it's a mask to cover the natural fear lurking just beneath the surface. The resulting shade and shape of their demeanor is that of resolve. There will be no stopping them.

"M. Get them as close as you can, but make sure they're safe. If you see anything, grab them and bail. Call me and let me know when you're in position, leaving, or if anything else happens." He's been on enough special operations missions to know what to do. I trust him at this point. "Jed, Jasmine. At the hint of anything funky, you get out of there. Got it?"

They nod back in agreement from inside the car. Then they're off. Andy and I burn through another cigarette in the courtyard and discuss the vicissitude of the previous six hours. One last hard drag. Extinguish the ember. Move forward. It's time to get back to the mission.

Andy and I spend the next couple of hours beside each of the stations, taking photos and observing the process. Eventually, we get on the tools, sew crooked lines into leather, spread glue, and produce the ugliest pair of footwear of the day. The Afghan workers make fun of us the entire way. Years of manual labor have enabled them to build a beautiful flip-flop within an hour of seeing the material. They make it look easy, as master craftsman often do. Our enthusiasm and playful naivety give them a never ending source for playful shit-talking.

This factory can build what we need. They have the crew, skills, and machinery to build the footwear. It's a math game at this point. What's their minimum run? Can they source material as well as produce? If so, what's the cost of the material and labor? As Andy and I huddle over the details, Jasmine and Jed return, somber.

Experiencing the fresh aftermath of a suicide bomber is life changing.

Crowds of people gather around a loose perimeter, frantically searching for friends and relatives. At first it doesn't make sense. It's a mess, a puzzle disassembled. Then you look for the divot in the ground. Patterns of shredded metal and debris expand in a flowerlike shape from that small hole at chaos center. Rubble, deformed earth, and fragments of human litter the ground.

It was a backpack bomb. Someone placed the explosives near a popular street vendor with the intent of taking advantage of the morning rush. Jed and Jasmine found what they were looking for up close, the seering stink of war.

I ask them if everything is okay.

"It was pretty rough," Jed replies. "I don't know how many people it got, but there was at least one kid that died."

He pulls the camera out of his bag, turns on the display screen, and scrolls through crisp images of men shoveling parts of a small child into a bucket. Reality framed in perfect depth of field, contrast, and color. One man's face, painted in a subtle shade of apathy, suggests such butchery is familiar in the streets where his children play. This is what we're fighting.

There are a multitude of skills the military teaches. Some are more transparent than others: marksmanship, concise communication, teamwork, problem solving in austere environments, physical fitness, punctuality, and more. Then there are other skills that are learned in a more innate fashion: adaptation, resilience, and the underappreciated yet overused art of compartmentalization.

When confronted, people generally go down one of two action paths: thinking or feeling. Thinking is objective and requires facts, data, and past experiences. Feeling is subjective and is capable of producing a physical response, from joyous laughter to abdominal crushing nausea. When operating in a dangerous environment, one is much more likely to get you killed than the other. Even in the worst moments imaginable, you can think your way out of a problem. However, walking into death is a lot more likely if you can't see through your own tears.

Weather intentional or not, the military teaches that the best course of action is to take those feelings, fold them up, put them in a mental box, close the lid, and toss them into a closet. Those feelings will not help you in a moment like this. They will only increase your chances of getting dead.

With the closet door closed, walk over to the box full of data, procedures, and grit. Rip the lid, and get to work. The path of thinking eventually becomes the way, the way of the fighter, survivor, and leader. Think first. Feel later, or not at all. The feelings of the day are already neatly folded, placed in boxes, and shoved in the closet by the time Jed turns off his camera. The group needs calm resolve, and somebody has to provide it.

It's time to go. Prior to leaving, the factory manager

agrees to pick up the faulty footwear at our compound and give them away to Afghans in need. They aren't worth the cost of shipping home, so they might as well go to good use on the streets of Kabul. It feels like the right thing to do given the circumstances of the day.

We shake hands, agree to follow up via email on the production details, and leave the factory. However, the initial numbers are not looking good. In addition to a higher production cost, we'll need to confirm an order of at least 20,000 pairs of flip-flops. We had a big day behind us and have a long one in front. Tomorrow, we head into the Panjshir Valley.

History buffs understand the significance of the Panjshir Valley. It was the one valley in Afghanistan that both the Russians and the Taliban failed to control. Buried in the Hindu Kush, the entrance is a ten mile river, cut through the mountains by millennia of fluid persistence. Jagged rock cliffs extend hundreds of vertical feet out of the river bed. The western side of the river has a double lane road cut up the length of the canyon. Rock on one side and a sheer drop to the raging river on the other. When you make it through the cut, the beauty and harshness of the Panjshir Valley becomes blatantly clear. Hundreds of Soviet tanks, armored personnel carriers, and helicopter bodies litter the valley floor in between rock and mud homes. This was the neighborhood of the national hero of Afghanistan, Ahmad

Shah Massoud—The Lion of Panjshir.

On a previous trip to Afghanistan, I met a retired Army Sergeant Major, working as an advisor to the Afghan military, named Paul. Paul is a mover, a shaker, and a get-'er-done kind of guy. During his time in service, he saw the potential in Afghanistan and returned to help Afghan businesses do work with the US Military and other foreign businesses. He helped secure lodging and security for a previous trip, where we'd become friends.

Massoud is a personal hero of mine. At the age of thirty-three, he united all the tribes of Afghanistan, lead the Mujahideen to defeat the Soviets, and helped end the Cold War. A total badass. Paul knew the Massoud family and was invited to the valley often for meetings and events. September 9 marks the day of Massoud's death, and the entire nation celebrates his leadership and iconic status.

Today is September 9. Paul had secured our team an invite to the official government ceremony at the Massoud Shrine in the Panjshir Valley. The plan is to depart early in the morning to avoid Kabul traffic, drive the three hours to the Panjshir Valley, attend the ceremony, spend the night in a guest home, and return the next morning.

We are in a two-vehicle 4Runner convoy. Our team of four and Paul with his three Panjshiri employees. Jasmine and I ride in Paul's vehicle, and Jed with Andy ride in the trail vehicle. At multiple points during the drive into Panjshir, Jed hangs his body out of the rear passenger window while Andy holds onto his legs and feet. The camera is pressed to his face while he films our vehicle rallying up the slot canyon. Despite the previous day's events, spirits are unpredictably high. And why shouldn't they be? After all, we're alive and moving forward on a grand adventure.

After what seems like an eternity, the valley begins to open up. As the floor widens, we immediately pull over to a small building alongside the creek. It's time to take a tea break. The crew exits the vehicles and enters the center door on the building. The first room looks like a roadside convenience store. Through the open windows in the back of the store, we can see individual tables, chairs, and blankets arranged next to the river. The proprietor leads us to tables, and shortly thereafter brings us tea and flatbread.

The natives observe our group but pay special attention to Andy. Comparatively, Andy is a fucking giant. He towers over groups of people in the United States, so his height is inconceivable to many of the locals. They've simply never seen a human being that tall before. Politely, they ask to take pictures. Afghan men, young and old, proudly take cell phone photos standing next to the Montana man. Smiles and laughs echo through the store.

It's early, so we have time before the festivities begin. One of the drivers wants to stop by his house, see his children, have us meet his father, and hang out by the river until the ceremony. As we leave the tea house, the beauty of the Panjshir Valley continues to reveal herself to us. The river spreads out across the valley floor, with orchards and crops lining the waterfront. Homes pucker the slopes and adjacent hillside draws. The terrain becomes more spectacular around every bend of the serpentine road. No wonder why no army could ever take this valley. I know I'd fight to the death to protect this slice of heaven.

We turn right off the main road to a small home alongside an almond orchard. This is the driver's house. His young daughter emerges from the home and waits by the road to hug her dad. The rest of the family follows after. Hugs all the way around.

"Are those rocket pods?" I ask one of drivers, pointing toward the large conical object 100 feet behind the house, nestled under the shade of an almond tree.

He makes the international hand and arm signal for a helicopter, stinger missile, and helicopter falling from the sky. Apparently that's a rocket pod from a Soviet attack helicopter that was left sitting for around twenty-five years. A quick scan of the property reveals more war scrap. Mostly helicopter parts—everywhere. What the hell happened here?

For the next two hours, the driver's father leads us around the property, telling tales of fighting the invaders from the hilltops and downing helicopters. By his count, he got thirteen of them, most of which fell in his backyard. This is easily the most impressive single-owner war trophy case I've ever seen. It's too irresistible not to photograph. Through the driver, we're able to translate to the father that we want to have him model our flip-flops while sitting on top of a rocket pod. Proudly, he accepts the role. The next thirty minutes consist of an ad hoc photoshoot with Muj fighters wearing flip-flops. You can't make this shit up.

Helicopters are flying overhead. They contain dignitaries from Kabul who have flown up for the ceremony. They're picking up in volume, indicating it's time for us to get moving. Hugs and smiles with the family and we're back in the Toyotas. It's another twenty minutes to the shrine.

The valley is so breathtaking that the time passes in an instant. Soon, we're being directed off the road toward event parking by Afghan Army road guards. Massoud's shrine sits atop a finger ridge that juts out into the valley. Overlooking the river, a large hexagonal monument with a forty-foot-tall dome top dominates the terrain features. The final resting place of the nation's hero.

As we exit the parking lot, the walkways leading to the shrine are lined with pictures of fallen Mujahideen fighters, martyrs for the nation. The volume of images is overwhelming. Thousands of men who died in the fight to preserve their valley. And today is their day of recognition.

The marching band lines up in front of the monument, and the ceremonial music begins. The next hour consists of talks, wreath laying, and moments of silence. It's an unforgettable experience to watch his family members, dignitaries, and fellow citizens pay homage to those who gave up their lives to protect their homeland.

"Griff. Want to check out Massoud's house?" Paul asks.

"His house?"

"It's like a museum now. They haven't touched anything in it since the day he passed. People are gathering there to pay respects to the family. Let's go check it out."

The chance to visit the home of a legend? Not only yes, but hell yes. The group makes its way back to the Toyotas, down the hill, and head north toward the Lion's home. We park on the steep driveway alongside twenty other vehicles and start walking toward the building. Paul leads the group and knows the name of virtually every person in the line leading to the garden alongside the home. Paul becomes more impressive by the minute.

Within five minutes, the group is seated in the garden with Massoud's brother and son. The feeling is surreal. Days ago, we were flying to Afghanistan to pick up flip-flops, and now we're sitting in the Lion of Panjshir's garden with his family. This is completely unexpected. I'm at a loss for words. What do you say to these guys?

Over the course of conversation, we learn Massoud's son attended the British Military Academy, Sandhurst. I attended the US Military Academy, so we start talking college experiences. He relays a story that will forever shape the direction of our company.

It's common for military academies to bring in officers returning from war to lecture cadets about the realities of warfare. During a lecture at Sandhurst, a senior officer discussed the war in Afghanistan. At one point in the lecture, the officer stated, "Afghans don't like visitors." Massoud's son sat in the audience and felt compelled to defend the reputation of his nation. During the question and answer section of the lecture, he was granted the opportunity to speak his piece.

"Sir, your statement about Afghans not liking visitors is not true. We love visitors. We don't like invaders."

That statement hits like a Mack truck. Visitors. Not invaders.

The conversation continues for a little longer, but the line leading into the garden is growing. It's time to go. We say our good-byes and head back to the vehicles. Lines of dignitaries extend down the long driveway.

We spend the rest of the afternoon touring the valley, taking photos, and drinking tea. An hour before sunset, we arrive at a guest house. The place smells of roasting lamb, rice, and fresh bread. For the next two hours, we feast over candlelight. Through open smiles and laughter, we discuss the epic nature of the day with gratitude.

The valley is too beautiful to not take advantage of the early morning light for photography and video. We agree to wake up early, take advantage of photo opportunities on our way out of valley, and exit the Panjshir toward Kabul by nine in the morning. After dinner, the team preps gear for a quick exit in the morning and hits the rack.

It's tough getting to sleep. Flashes of a child being shoveled into a bucket. The faces of the martyrs. The depths of their sacrifices. Overwhelming images of pain. Once you see it, you can't unsee it. Your scale is forever altered.

They lost thousands of people. We've lost thousands of flip-flops. Our problems feel benign.

We wake up before daybreak and head down the valley under the guidance of headlights. We have about two hours of good working light for Jed and Jasmine. Jed leads the charge and picks out spots for landscape imagery. Drive for ten minutes. Dismount. Film. Load up. Repeat. During one of the stops, I observe a group of little girls wearing white head dressings, peppering the mountainside. The photo shoots continue all the way down to the tea house now famous for hosting the tallest white guy in Afghanistan. With the last bit of tea onboard, the 4Runners enter the slot canyon leading to the valley below. Cell phone coverage is spotty in the Panjshir, but it is non-existent in the canyon. The terrain is too tight for any signal.

We pass the last checkpoint on the way out of the valley, and the burner phone vibrates. A message. It's Walt from Commerce. We need to call him back immediately.

"Walt. Got your call. What's up?"

"I got a hold of that factory near the military training center. They'd like to meet with you."

"When?"

"This afternoon. Can you make it here by noon?"

"That's going to be tight. We still need to make the drive to Kabul and get through morning traffic."

"See you there."

We have to roll. Calls between the vehicles confirm that we need fuel and a bite to eat to make the drive back unimpeded. There's a gas station in the next village. We can likely get food while the trucks are filling up. The team agrees to make it fast. As the drivers fill the trucks, we observe an older Afghan man hobbling down the road with a stack of flatbread in his arms. Andy and I make the approach. This will need to be hand and arm signal engagement—neither of us know the language. At the sight of a twenty dollar bill, the gentleman gladly hands over the entire stack of bread to Andy, smiles, and takes the cash. We probably paid twenty bucks for three dollars' worth of bread. Who cares? We have to roll.

The timeline seems to provide the drivers with a mission. They want to make the hit time. And each one of them wants to be first. The next three hours consists of loud music, dusty passes, and "alternate" routes through Kabul. Over the course of four deployments, I've been a part of hundreds of ground movements. Only one of those movements was scarier than this ride. The drivers rip through pothole-laden streets, narrowly missing other cars, bicyclists, and roadside vendors. There is no stopping them. All we can do is hang on and be fully present in the adventure.

We make it. Almost. We're half an hour late, but given the circumstances and distance traveled, it's impressive. There is no time to change. Andy and I are dropped off at the the meeting in T-shirts, jeans, and hoodies. The other vehicle takes Jasmine and Jed back to the compound.

Walt meets us at the gate and escorts us in. We are way underdressed. All of the executives of the factory are present, in suits, in front of a lunch that was supposed to be served thirty minutes earlier. Not the best first impression.

Over the course of the meal, we do the standard introductions and outline the company background and work desired. We learn this factory just invested over a million dollars into injection molding equipment and assembly machinery. It's the most advanced footwear factory in Afghanistan. They're working on a 180,000 pair boot order for the Afghan National Army and would be in production for the next eight months. There's plenty of time to get our production rolling. The excitement is building, and we're itching to see the factory floor.

I find myself staring again. This time, mouth slightly open, jaw down. This factory is bigger than John's. It's roughly the same size as factory number two, but is closer equipped to the best footwear factory images we'd found on Google. Instead of workers wearing white coats and face masks, women wear purple burkas and men wear industrial uniforms. They are everywhere, surrounded by flat tables with stacks of boot material, operating levers on a twenty-foot, circular injection molding monstrosity, packing boots into boxes. It's beautiful. We're back in business.

After the factory tour, both parties agree to follow up on the details, the timeline to reproduce the defective footwear, and the sampling process. Smiles and hugs all the way around before we depart.

M is waiting in the parking lot. the Kabul Military Training Center sign is directly in front of us, as we exit. A group of military instructors march around young Afghan men. Gaggles of teenagers in mismatched uniforms are being molding into a military machine that mirrors the equipment, structure, and leadership of the armies that have failed throughout time in Afghanistan. It didn't make sense, yet made perfect sense.

A professional military is glutinous for guns, bullets, gear, and fuel. It is an industry all its own. In 2003, the Afghan National Army had 1,750 professional soldiers. There are over 200,000 now. Each of those 200,000 soldiers make under $1,900 a year at the cost of roughly $46,000 annually. The cost to equip those 200,000 soldiers is over $14,300 each. The US taxpayer bears virtually all of those costs, adding up to more than $3.5 billion a year. Quick math. You, the US taxpayer are paying more than seven and a half times what it would cost to educate every child in Afghanistan, on training and equipping the Afghan National Army in tactics that have historically not been successful in Afghanistan. All the while, most of the soldiers being trained are illiterate themselves, making most of the costly training even less effective. We are paying an egregious amount teaching people how to march in rows and columns instead of teaching them how to read and write.

The new factory is ready to work. It's all up to the math now. *How much will replacement materials cost to remake the first run? How much cash do we have in the bank account? How many returns has Lee issued after the email?*

"Lee, we found a new factory and can get the flip-flops remade. We need to know how much cash you refunded after the email."

"About $200."

"What? That's like three orders."

"Yeah. The response to your email has been awesome. People are down to wait."

They haven't given up on us. Thousands of people want to see this happen. They've paid seventy dollars for a pair of flip-flops, but they've ended up buying a front-row seat to an entrepreneurial adventure. They've seen how far we are willing to go at this point. What would make them doubt that we wouldn't see it through?

Despite the reassuring news, we're roughly $20,000 short between what's left in the bank and the cost of materials.

What do you do when you're going through hell? You keep going.

As a business owner and entrepreneur, you have to take risks. I've been a military and working professional for nearly twelve years. Worked, earned, paid bills, bought a car, owned a home—all of that stuff required to get an acceptable credit score and irresponsible credit card limit. 1-800-531-2265. The USAA Federal Savings Bank customer service hotline. I've been calling this number since I was fourteen and know that someone will answer the call, listen to my problem, and help me fix it.

"Hi. I am going to be placing two large charges across my card to purchase materials for my company."

The USAA Representative responds in the upbeat, professional tone I've become accustomed to. "Sure thing, Captain Griffin. I'll make a note on your account and make sure they go through."

And it's done. Materials are back in production. We see the path forward to redemption. For the remainder of the evening, we sit at the courtyard table, smoking, laughing, talking, and staring into the changing evening temperature. We're gone tomorrow.

In addition to our original luggage, we load two duffel bags filled with the defective footwear, stuffed in opium sacks, into the car

There's a line from Jack Kerouac's book, *On the Road*,

that I've always taken with me. "You can get anywhere in the world with a pack of smokes, a lighter, and a smile." Around the world, that holds true. The plastic poly wrap bags are loaded into the bottom of the duffel with a few sacrificial flip-flops open and left on top. The final touch is a few unopened packs of Marlboro Lights, placed on top too.

Getting to the airport demands multiple security checkpoints and searches. The vehicles are initially swept for bombs with mirrors and dogs. All bags are unloaded and sent through a security shack filled with X-ray equipment and men with machine guns. Airport security in Kabul is not a joke.

The personal bags and camera equipment go first without issue, then the duffels. Without hesitation, the guy behind the screen yells to his friend, and the bags are grabbed as they exit the X-ray machine. We stand opposite two young Afghan security guards as they slide the bags onto a metal table, directing us to open them. The process is simple. Stand there, wait for them to rifle through the bag, do a swipe, and then they stare at you. Big smile, removal of the flip-flops and smokes off the top and onto the table, then zip the bag closed. You can get anywhere in the world with a pack of smokes, a lighter, and a smile.

It's time to say goodbye to M. He's provided so much to us: time, direction, humor, and most importantly, safety. The team's gratitude for him is incalculable. After hugs and commitment to be friends on Facebook, his Corolla exits the parking lot back onto the streets of Kabul.

When you depart a war zone on good terms, there's an

invisible twenty-pound vest lifted from your shoulders that you've grown accustomed to wearing. It's the ever present, subtle, yet imposing weight of responsibility to keep your team and yourself from dying. It's a weight I'm grateful I get to sluff off, embarking for safer pastures.

The trip home is a blur. The weight of the week begins to set in. We disconnect in our own ways, taking advantage of just being able to sit, stare, and know we did something meaningful this week.

Kabul to Dubai. Dubai to Amsterdam. Amsterdam to Seattle. 11 September 2012, we are home, exhausted. Eleven years to the day after the tragic events that changed so many lives, we return home from the war zone again. In less than ninety-six hours, a transition is made from dust, danger, and death to a birthday cake with candles on the dining room table. It's my daughter's eighth birthday.

She could have been the kid in that bucket. Those boxes, the ones stuffed to the brim with emotions and packed away, seem to fall from the back shelf and open themselves up inside of you at their convenience. The reality we carry does not coincide with the reality we occupy after stepping off those flights. The choice is, there is no choice. Swallow it. Shove it down. Cram another piece of yourself back into the festering box. Smile. Here comes the cake.

Happy birthday to you! Happy birthday to you!

Chapter VI
-Garage Days-

September quickly yields to October. Andy and the new factory correspond weekly via Skype calls to coordinate the sample materials, specifications, timelines, and logistics to get the new run of materials from China to Kabul. Things are going smoothly. Customers are satisfied with our level of communication, and we can see light at the end of the tunnel. The materials will be in a container on their way to Afghanistan by the first week of December, and ready for production by mid-to-late January. They estimate a month of production time, then shipment to the US and Europe. We'll be delivering footwear mid-March of 2013.

From the launch of the website to delivery is fifteen months. Thousands of people wait over a year for us to make good on our promises. In a world of instant-satisfaction, it feels as foreign as it does inspiring. Forward-thinking, like-minded problem solvers send us motivational emails, posts on social media, and make phone calls. The messages can be paraphrased:

Go get 'em. Get after it.

They believe. In doing so, they made us believe. We wanted to quit so many times. Their words of encouragement kept us in the fight.

Two weeks from the container shipment to Afghanistan. The factory goes dark. They stop answering the phone. No email response. No Skype responses either. Is everything OK? This goes on for over a week until the nervousness reaches an actionable level.

In the course of our discussions with the manufacturer, we'd coordinated schedules across the eleven-and-a-half-hour time zone difference. There were certain windows to talk when both teams were awake. During one of the discussions, I learned the director of operations had a weekly call with his advisory board via Skype. There it is on the calendar. The only option is to stay up for a late Skype text session. We know he'll be online and won't be able to ignore the tones of my incoming messages on top of the board call. At least we'll know they've received our communication.

His icon is active. Time to start sending messages. He responds immediately in the text box. He'll need a few minutes on the call, and then will type his response from the board. The next few minutes are filled with silent thoughts of potential disasters. His response finally comes.

```
The factory had its boot contract pulled
and had to cease production immediately.
To keep the factory open, you'll need to
    provide a contractual commitment to
  purchase 80,000 flip-flops annually.
```

Eighty thousand? We can barely make four thousand. The remainder of the Skype text conversation is short.

We thank him for the opportunity to work with the factory and will have an answer back in the next few days. I have to call Lee.

"Lee. Bad news. The factory closed."

"What. The. Fuck? What are we going to do?"

"I don't know."

It's time to close the laptop and tell Michele. I've lost count of the massive failures along the long road in pursuit of this dream. The credit cards are completely maxed. With Christmas in less than a month, it's going to be another thin year.

Whatever your spiritual beliefs, you're here to learn lessons. While your spirit lives in a mass of meat and bones, the universe provides you challenges, lessons, and inspiration to grow. It rarely gives you what you want, rather provides you what you need. Whatever happens to you is the best possible thing that could have happened to you. In fact, it's the only thing that could have happened.

For the next few days, we war-game all possible courses of action to turn that container full of flip-flop material into finished footwear. We already own the materials. Might as well finish the job. We call boutique to large footwear manufacturers. The run is either too small, can't be fit into production before spring, or is too expensive. We're burning through solutions as quickly as we can come up with them.

Andy is in his car on Capitol Hill in Seattle. Lee is in LA. I'm at my dining room table. Through the cell phone conference call, we discuss the bad news.

What do you do when you're going through hell? You keep going.

There are those moments of melee when a good friend says something to fully remind you why you're such good friends to begin with. "Fuck it," Andy chimes in. "I'll make them."

"What?" echoed from both Lee and me.

"We saw them made in Kabul. The process didn't look complicated. We can do it."

"You're kidding, right?"

"No. We can do it."

The enthusiasm is all fine and good, but where are we going to make 4,000 pairs of flip-flops? We don't have money to rent a building. Where will the tools come from? How do we get a container shipped to Seattle? Logistics, the professionals, start talking.

Andy goes into Tasmaniana overdrive. Using production skills and a network built over his twenty years in the construction and manufacturing industry, the Wookie begins putting the pieces together. Tools, glue, presses, and a sander. Add a couple of industrial tables and we'll have a flip-flop production facility. It's not much. It can likely fit in a garage. I have a garage. Why not, right? A lot can be accomplished in six hundred square feet of dimly lit shack. It doesn't quite have the curbside appeal of the last factory we were in, but it's what we have, and that's enough for us.

When I bought the home, it was a dilapidated carport. Over the years, walls, siding, and doors were installed to make it a secure garage. Our factory is filled with memorabilia: christmas ornaments, halloween decorations, mountain bikes, tools, and everything else not welcome in a living space. There has always been the dream of turning it into a man cave, but finances and the pace of life never permitted the transformation. It isn't the male retreat space I've previously envisioned, but I like the idea a whole lot more than letting down all of those people who believe in us.

Andy works with a gentleman named Scott at Snowboard Connection in downtown Seattle. Scott is an engineer, through and through. He worked his way through the Seattle aviation community and manages a facility for an avionics manufacturing company. It's his job to make sure the building is functional, the equipment runs appropriately, and that everything hums for the technicians to crank out products. In a fortuitous series of events, the company is moving from a 40,000- square-foot facility to a much larger building. They have piles of older equipment that are going to scrap or to a massive sale. Based on his discussions with Andy, Scott's engineer brain pieces together the tool list required to make it work—out of a pile of discarded equipment.

Stacks of fluorescent light fixtures. Dented conference room tabletops. Small vacuum pumps. Ovens. Plastic bins. All that is missing is the sander and the dust collector. During the month of December, the garage is emptied, painted, floor epoxied, wired for power, and built into a guerilla flip-flop factory. Friends and family show up seven days a week to help paint, run wire, level tabletops, and organize. Andy gets smart on adhesives and orders buckets of water-based glues. The sander and dust collectors are installed. We're ready.

I can only imagine what the truck driver thinks as he hauls the twenty-foot steel shipping container into a quaint neighborhood and stops in front of a single-story building with two men standing in front of the open garage doors, the tall one holding a bottle of champagne.

Andy greets the driver with a friendly request. "Hey, man, can you pull the truck forward a little bit? We need to break this bottle over the back of the container."

"Um, sure."

Wearing his favorite "Billy Hill for Sheriff" T-shirt, Andy cracks the bottle over the rear corner of the container. Broken glass meets with bubbles and a triumphant cheer. Now finally, after all these long months of horseplay, we can get to work. The doors swing open. The container is full. Knowing the volume of materials, the first loads of boxes are put on a trailer and shuttled to Andy's garage across town. The next wave of boxes go into the old motorhome sitting in my driveway. Stacks on top of stacks on top of the bed in the back, the floor, the couch, the bunk bed, and every chair. The motorhome used for numerous family adventures is now the home of hundreds of unassembled flip-flops. The remainder of the boxes goes into the Combat Flip Flops production facility.

Andy has the plan. Prior to going into full swing production, we need to test the process. For the next few days, the team works to figure out the right process to mix glues, create application procedures, find the flow of materials through the shop, and the correct movement of the finished flip-flop across the sander. Boxes are organized by style, size, and production schedule.

Lee flies in from Los Angeles. Family flows between the kitchen and the garage. Five or six veteran friends pull into the driveway. Jed drives out from Spokane to film.

Pair #1.

AK-47. Size 9. Serial #0000000000000001

We share the smiles, hugs, and tears of the long and arduous road that has led us to this new beginning. The first pair is boxed and placed on the shelf. The celebration is as brief as it is necessary. There is work to be done.

The next few months blur together. Five a.m. wake-up. Step out to the garage to run the heater, then return to the kitchen for a cup of coffee. In a slightly less than slightly conscious state, strap on the respirator, start priming the rubber outsoles laid out by Andy the night prior. By 6:30 a.m., the outsoles are stacked in boxes, and the process is repeated for the mating surfaces of the mid-layers and heel wedges.

By the time Andy arrives in the shop, he can start punching the thong portion through layers of stacked materials, apply glue, heat activate the glue in the oven, do the layup, and shove the flip-flop into the vacuum press. After being removed from the vacuum press, they are stacked in plastic bins and placed in front of the sander. By mid-afternoon, Andy shifts to the sander and begins smoothing out the rough edges. Then back into bins and placed onto the shipping table.

Blessed with compressed air, the flip-flops are placed into the box with a hand-signed letter and a piece of Bazooka bubble gum. The garage factory echoes the cacophony of tape guns, and shipping label printer sounds. Boxes begin to pile up by the shipping door. Then they are gone.

Out into the world and onto the feet of the new revolutionaries. Images of smiling customers come through email, Facebook, and text messages. Fifteen months late, they are smiling and telling the story of Business, Not Bullets.

We need help. Even working all day every day, there is no way we could finish 4,000 pairs by summer with only two people.

Another interesting friend of Andy's who we've enlisted into the Unarmed Forces is David Van Dyke, also known as "DVD." He has a soft spot for fast bikes and charges the mountains like a boss. He has a flexible work schedule. Everyday, for months, he drives to the shop to help.

Jimmy Settle, Also known as, "Jimmy", is a native Alaskan who recently separated from the Air Force as a Pararescueman. Jimmy has short hair, a huge smile, and a tattoo of the Cheshire Cat in a Pararescue beret—smoking a joint—seven of the nine lives crossed out in the smoke. In military circles, he's what they call a "Shit Magnet." We can go on about Jimmy, but you should just read his book, *Never Quit*. Jimmy parks his motorhome in the driveway adjacent to to the flip-flop factory and doesn't leave until the work is finished.

Ater work, Andy's wife and daughter, Kristy and Taylor, respectively, will help detail the footwear and package the goods for shipping. My wife, Michele, and my daughters,

Estella and Amelia, fold hundreds of footwear boxes nightly, holding competitions to see who can make the tallest pile of boxes.

A state of family flow. It isn't easy, but backed with good beats, a sense humor, and an occasional White Russian for morale, the run is done. All of the footwear is distributed. America, Europe, Canada, Australia, Africa.

The moment the final pair of flip-flops from the initial order shipped was a welcome triumph for the Unarmed Forces. If you're reading this as one of the first believers—Thank you. From the bottom of our hearts, we can't express the gratitude felt for your faith, trust, and patience. You could have given up on us, but you didn't. So we couldn't give up on you either. Everything from that moment forward was the result of your actions.

Through countless challenges, the movement had come a long way from idea, to spoken word, to digital rendering, to physical form, to frustration, to adaptation, to delivery. The Unarmed Forces never surrendered, and we won a decisive battle, but we had yet to successfully complete the mission.

The Mission: create peaceful, forward-thinking opportunities for self-determined entrepreneurs affected by conflict. Our willingness to take bold risks, community connection, and distinct designs communicating, "Business, Not Bullets," flipping the view on how wars are won.

Through persistence, creativity, and respect, we will empower the mindful consumer to manufacture peace through trade.

We were at a crucial juncture. Continuing the present strategy of manufacturing flip-flops in Afghanistan seemed about as silly as continuing to throw bombs at the country year after year and hope the situation would improve. Remember what Einstein said, "Insanity is doing the same thing over and over again and expecting different results." It was time to put our own advice to work. We need to shift perspective, direction, and consciousness if we were to be victorious.

- PART II -
RISE

Chapter VII
-Visions of White-

Awake with the quiet hours. Before the gallop of tiny feet meet the day.

They're not old enough yet to understand, to be burdened by the weight of the world. How beautiful, how prestine that naïvety. How long can we shelter our children from the failures and misdeeds of our generation? How do we teach them to not fall into the predictable patterns of their predecessors?

The perfect chaos of morning begins at the end of these questions and long before their answers. Breakfast is prepared. Lunches are laid out to be packed into tiny school bags. The first beams of early morning sunlight shine through open windows, illuminating the day ahead.

We walk together toward their school, as other children and families step out into the world. Just like us, they make the slow stroll down 2nd Avenue. The kids call to each other. Adults give nods of recognition in between sips of coffee. The stream of youth funnels onto the single sidewalk leading up the slow hill to the elementary school. Hundreds of children on the only path they know.

Busses unload, and parents drop kids in the assigned area.

The sidewalk is too crowded for a sincere good-bye. The previous two weeks were filled with travel, stress, anxiety, death, hope, and exhaustion. The look on their faces, peck on the cheek, and a gentle embrace make it all worthwhile.

"See ya, Dad."

"What? No hug and kiss?"

"Dad, don't embarrass me. There's lots of people around."

"If you don't do it, I'm going to sing. You know I will." Breaking into tones only made possible by ears deafened by gunfire, lack of interest in music class, and a desire for complete embarrassment, I follow through. "YOU ARE MY SUNSHINE. MY ONLY SUNSHINE. YOU MAKE ME HAPPY—"

"Fine." She complies with a quick hug and kiss.

"I love you. Have a great day at school."

As she walks toward the door, a vivid memory grips my throat and yanks me one week into the past. Lucid as that September morning, I can see the hillside school in the Panjshir Valley, placed perfectly on the side of the steep slope. A single-story building constructed in an "L" shape inside of a standard Afghan walled compound. A black metal access gate with a single door open in the lower right side. A few kilometers behind the building, a panorama of the Hindu Kush. Outlines of white rocks marking the terrain, polluted with landmines leftover from the war with Russia. Terrain that will never be walked on again without fear.

Those white rocks stood out in contrast against the brown and sage terrain. A clear marker that said, "Don't step foot in here. We'll blow your shit up when you least expect it." It was a common sight throughout Afghanistan, but they really popped in the early morning sun.

White hijabs stood bright on the hillside, spread out across fifty yards. Some in gaggles, others a little farther apart. Little girls beaming like the future on the remote slope. They didn't want to go sit in a classroom for hours. They'd rather be outside playing in nature, just being kids.

The old man in the white Corolla, I remember so clearly. He had the Toyota nose down on a bumpy twenty-degree slope. The car bounced with precision. A skill learned from years of driving low clearance sedans on the roughest terrain on the planet. He was fifteen yards from the girls who were farthest from the door, and closing. They ran from him.

Then he stopped, flung the door open, stepped out, and leaned over the top of the car while waving at the girls. I imagined the exchange going something like this:

"But Dad, I don't want to go to school. It's so boring."

"Look, I just drove you and the rest of the girls from the village ten kilometers down the road. Get out. Time for you to go to school."

"But Dad."

"Out. I love you."

As they tended to be, the young girls were distracted. Kids are kids.

I can hear the thoughts of her father as if they were my own. *I told her to get to school. The bell is going to ring. She's going to be late. What is she doing? Doesn't she know girls like her couldn't go to school a few years ago? I'll show her.*

I watch him yank the steering wheel, pulling the car off

the road and down the slope across the hill. He laughed while using years of herding experience to move the girls toward the opening in the big metal gate.

I could hear her thoughts as though they were my daughter's, *My dad is so embarrassing. Is he really driving his car down the hill after us?*

He continued giggling, knowing just how much he's embarrassing his daughter, then stops, opens the door, and pops out. At the top of his voice, "I LOVE YOU HONEY. HAVE A GREAT DAY AT SCHOOL."

She shrugged in embarrassment, turned her back, and headed toward her future. She may not have known it, but he did.

The community pulled off an epic feat of entrepreneurial insanity; however, we weren't any closer to victory than when we started the mission. We had a few thousand left in the bank account, but it was clear the company was on the brink of failure. In many ways, we were actually worse off than when we started. All of the factories were closed, and we'd burned though most of our industry contacts.

As hard as we fought to get the initial flip-flops out the door, it didn't help stave the problems we were trying solve. Employment. War. A lack of empathy. We managed to save our own asses from having to work off years of debt created by a small business, but we failed to make the change that inspired the customers. No working Afghan factories. No families employed. No American Dream.

After every training exercise or mission executed in the military, there's an After Action Review (AAR). The AAR is an opportunity to discuss what you did right, what you did wrong, what to sustain, and what to improve upon. It's a formal process that happens right after you shed your gear, store your weapons, and grab a quick bite to eat. Leaders stand up and go through every aspect of the mission. Were the maps right? Did the breach go smoothly? Did we have the right gear to exploit the target? Significant details of the mission are highlighted, documented, and marked for improvement where needed.

After eighteen months of developing products, marketing, failing, selling, failing, shipping, failing, producing, failing, and eventually delivering, we needed an AAR. It was time to take an honest look at the business, highlight what we did right and what we did wrong.

Why didn't it work? Why couldn't we keep the factories open? Why weren't people latching onto this mission and supporting it in droves? Who wouldn't want to support a veteran-owned company making flip-flops in Afghanistan to create positive social change? Did we mess up on the messaging? Was the pricing too high? Did the products suck?

The war still raged, fueled by an endless supply of tax dollars, fear, and a customer apathetic to the outcome. It just keeps going and going. Our friends continue to deploy, returning home injured or in flag-draped boxes, and the media keeps repeating the same sad thirty second stories about the fallen or injured. Social media only amplifies the failures. Day after day. Images of Rangers in body armor holding a rifle, full of machismo, with a date, name, and province in the headline. Families crushed. Communities hurting.

As a nation, we aren't done. We continue to throw billions of dollars, thousands of souls, and our national pride at a problem impossible to solve through warfare. Why do we do this as a nation? Because it's the way we know?

I learned an invaluable lesson on my first deployment to Afghanistan. Our interpreter, Mustafa, provided directions to a contact in an adjacent village. We needed to get from point A to point B. As military leaders, we immediately went to the map and translated the directions onto printed terrain. We immediately noticed something wasn't right.

"I think your directions are messed up, Mustafa. You're telling us to go to the south, but there is a road to the north that's half the distance. Why are we going the long way?"

"That's the way to the village."

"Yeah, that's definitely a route to the village, but it's twice as long."

"Because that's the way to the village."

In an effort to prove common sense and years of military training correct, the conversation continued for another five minutes. Fingers pointed at a line on a map. Reference to the scale in the legend to mark out the distance of the respective routes. Simple discussion of what's shorter, five miles or ten miles? Simple shit that would have driven anybody with common sense crazy.

Finally, the Chaplain chimed in, "Hey Griff, what's the shortest distance between two points?"

My answer came with arrogance of an engineering degree and years of land navigation courses. "It's a straight fucking line."

"Not here. It's the way you know."

He was right. Habit is a motherfucker. Even though a better, shorter solution to a problem is offered and right in front of us, years of cultural norms create a seemingly inefficient behavior. People don't change overnight. They take the same, comfortable route between where they are and where they want to be. It's worked for years, why shake anything up? If you know how to get something done, keep doing it that way until it fails. Point A to Point B via the way you know.

As a nation, we're failing. We aren't any closer to finishing the war than when we started, yet we continue to shovel holes in the Graveyard of Empires—history be damned. The simple truth is, you can't get to point B in Afghanistan through conventional warfare.

As a company, we were failing. We weren't any closer to keeping Afghans employed than when we started, yet we couldn't stop. Our friends kept coming home in boxes. The drive to create a solution only increased. We felt more compelled than ever to find a more efficient and sustainable route toward point B.

So it was time to do the AAR. In the months that existed between that container covered in champagne bubbles and the shipment of the flip-flops, there was plenty of time to discuss the infinite number of failures, mistakes, and things never to be done again. The entire team replayed the situation and timeline over and over again in between the sound of beats and vacuum presses.

The Price: $70
1. Too High.
2. The nearest competitor for a boutique, all leather flip-flop was $50. They were in all the resorts, had pro surfers repping the brand, and had magazine pages full of brazilian butt shots.
3. Who was gonna spend $20 more to get a pair of flip-flops off the internet, from an unknown company to put Afghans to work? Very few people.
4. The price had to come down.

Price Reduction:
1. Making products in Afghanistan was expensive. Credit is Haram (illegal per the Koran) in Islamic culture, so working capital used in the Western world wasn't applicable. It was all done in cash. That was expensive.
2. Raw materials couldn't be purchased in country. Afghanistan didn't have reliable leather tanneries, EVA-extruding facilities, or rubber trees. All the materials had to be purchased outside the borders and shipped in. Logistics costs plus import tariffs. Expensive.
3. Shipping to the United States from Kabul. It was

nearly the same price as the cost of the materials, tariffs, and labor combined. Add the sting of an import tariff—ouch. More expenses.

4. Review all the receipts and costs. "Keystone" math for retail margins for the manufacturers and dealers dictated a $130 price point. The receipts communicated a price reduction as impossible.

The Mission:

1. Seemed pretty clear. It was right there on the website. Those who read it understood it.

2. Media seemed to like the story but struggled to maintain traction past a few hours after a video drop or print article.

3. There wasn't a massive viral uptick in social media. The "share" button often went unused on the Facebook posts.

4. In between cats riding on robot vacuums and political rhetoric, thumbs scrolled right past the mission.

5. Did people really not care about jobs?

6. Were they satisfied with the known path, established in 1945 after claiming a World title? Bomb your enemy into submission, support the troops, and bam—freedom for all. Did people still believe that?

The Business:

1. All of the assumptions were wrong.
2. The costs exceeded expectations by a long shot.
3. Managing footwear production with no experience in the industry across multiple countries and a war zone proved to be slightly challenging.
4. There weren't any more open factories in Afghanistan.
5. We couldn't keep making flip-flops in the garage indefinitely. Even if we could, it was contrary to the mission, and the neighbors wouldn't put up with it much longer.

A successful person is often their own toughest critic. It's easy to trap to fall into to identify who you are as a person with your success or failure as an employee, business owner, or leader. After nearly two years of constant failures, it was easy to take on the role of failure. Cash was low. Morale was low. Product was low. Self esteem—low.

Just because your business is failing doesn't mean that you're a failure. One bad conversation with your spouse doesn't mean you're a bad spouse. One bad presentation to the big boss doesn't determine the rest of your career. What you did failed, but you have the ability to make a change moving forward. All that said, we had a difficult time seeing the next move.

Maybe it was the guy who requested a squid fighting a unicorn drawn on the receipt. Maybe it was the Navy SEALs sending photos of their Poseidons on exotic beaches. Maybe it was the letters from the family members of the fallen. The positive communication hit the inbox every day. Every time they did, the mission felt like less of a failure.

The messages and requests kept piling in. The positivity was palpable. A community of people began to interact on social media. It was small, but it was happening. Posts here. Shares there. Reposts. The previous year-and-a-half had left our small team exhausted. As soon as our fatigue began to slow our pace, the Unarmed Forces stepped in and drove the mission forward.

Military men have the impressive ability to communicate in a series of grunts, hand and arm signals, and movie quotes. The quote that continued to bounce around came from Mel Gibson in *The Patriot*, "Aim small, miss small." We aimed big and missed big.

We tend to imagine businesses starting like they do on television—rapid scale, smiles, and immediate social and economic impact. But revolutions don't start that way. They start with small numbers. They start with believers who are willing to step outside of their comfort zone to make change happen.

In the madness of the series of Afghan factory debacles and Operation Guerilla Garage, we couldn't see the scale of the community forming around the mission. Small groups of people dispersed across the US and Europe who spread the flames of what we call, "stoke." Stoke is an emotion that encourages and incites. People were encouraged to take a risk on a pair of flip-flops to prove a point. The delivery of the first run incited them to press forward and tell others, thereby, spreading stoke.

One of the many valuable lessons learned in Ranger School is right when you believe you are finished, you're really only about 10% of the way there. Through each phase of the training, the finish line seems to take a step back for each step forward. It requires you to keep putting one foot in front of the other, no matter how tired or broken you feel, until you're either medically dropped from participation or you're dead (another medical condition). You never quit on the mission. The little dose of stoke being fed back to us from the Unarmed Forces reminded us that we needed to display intestinal fortitude.

Five months prior to shipping that guerilla flip-flop run, the company put a $10,000 deposit on the PLATFORM Shoe Show in Las Vegas. With the second Afghan factory option still on the table, we thought it would be a good idea to attend the world's biggest shoe show, sell to dealers, save the mission, and get back on track of being the hottest footwear company on the market (It's okay to laugh, but optimism is more powerful than any bomb). After the factory closed and moved production to Washington, we had a tough decision to make. Go or no-go? The deposit wasn't refundable. Vegas had been good to us before. The team made the call. Go.

With garage flip-flop production in full swing and orders still hitting the website, Andy and I spent evenings constructing a tradeshow booth. Very Apple. White walls, big logo across the back, bright lights, and pillars artistically positioned flip-flops in front of custom-formed aluminum poppies. All of it fit in a 4'x4'x8' container on casters—in Seattle.

Andy was still working at his paint company. Lee was in Los Angeles doing design work. I was in Seattle. The timing only permitted for a solo mission in a Budget rental truck. Seattle to Vegas was a long way.

Small businesses are always family businesses. I love working alongside my loved ones. Buck being no exception. Buck is a seventy-two-year-old lifetime servant leader. He's also my father-in-law. He doesn't have an off button. When he heard about the impending road trip, he called me immediately and offered to come along.

Less than twelve hours later, the Budget truck rolled east down I-90 over the Cascades. With early mornings in the flip-flop factory and late nights with the tradeshow booth, the stress and exhaustion began to set in as the sun went down. I was smoked, so Buck offered to take the helm.

In his twenties, Buck served in the Peace Corps in South America. On one of his mission trips, he contracted a parasite that affected his vision. Through surgical procedures, he regained vision and carried on like a boss through life with bosslike glasses. This seventy-two-year-old man with questionable depth perception pinned his right foot to the floor and made sure those Panjshiri Afghans weren't going to beat him on the scariest ride roster. The thoughts bounced around my head: *I've lived fairly well. Good school. Awesome wife. Great kids. Done OK in business. Dying in a rental truck on a mountain pass driving a flip-flops trade show booth to Vegas, not the worst way to go.*

Thankfully, we made it to Vegas in time for the show. Lee drove in from Los Angeles, and Andy flew down from

Seattle. The merry trio was finally together in Sin City. Lee and Andy helped get the truck to the front of the forklift line and unloaded onto the floor.

We'd seen the booth space on the map, and it looked decent. We couldn't afford an expensive booth space near the entrance, but our budget real estate landed us close to a bar and bathrooms. As long as we were near traffic, the booth was going to beam, and people would buy flip-flops.

Nope.

Within the first few hours, we'd seen less than twenty people even walk in front of the booth. Vendors were conversing with each other across aisles, taking smoke breaks, and generally demonstrating frustrated boredom at a professional level. The realization the show was going to be a bust quickly set in. Ten thousand dollars spent on the booth space. Another thousand on the booth. Plane tickets. Rental truck. Zero Sales.

Fuck.

Andy is consistently and by far the most prepared and professional member of our team. Prior to arriving at the show, he understood a large portion of the event dealt with sourcing, i.e. the materials that go into the shoes. The sales reps would be selling the products on the floor, but the shoe designers were also at the show to find materials, manufacturers, and importers to build their designs. It was a shoe show from fiber to finished product. With order and requests continuing to pile in and materials running out, Andy was on a mission to find more production. "Guys, you need to check out the Colombian footwear. It's sick. Great leather. Quality assemble AND they have a free trade agreement with the US"

Over the course of the next two days, Colombian representatives floated through the booth to check out Combat Flip Flops. They could make the material, facilitate assembly, and ship in small runs. Without committing on price, they put forward numbers that made sense to get products to market for $50, barely. If we kept overhead low and focused on web sales, it was possible to deliver flip-flops to the US at a competitive price, barely. But did that fit the mission?

The Mission: *To create peaceful, forward-thinking opportunities for self-determined entrepreneurs affected by conflict. Our willingness to take bold risks, community connection, and distinct designs communicate, "Business, Not Bullets"—flipping the view on how wars are won. Through persistence, respect, and creativity, we empower the mindful consumer to manufacture peace through trade.*

It didn't say anything about Afghanistan. It said help entrepreneurs affected by conflict. Enable the mindful manufacturer to manufacture peace through trade. Colombia fit the mission.

Remember that War on Drugs? The narco-financed insurgency in Colombia that raged for decades, enslaved populations to the drug trade, and sucked up billions of dollars in US taxpayer money? Yeah, that one.

In our discussions with the Colombian reps, they explained how the economy was turning the tide in Colombia. Years of targeted military efforts put the FARC on its heels. To capitalize on the gains, the government granted amnesty to those who put down their arms, funded education programs, and promoted business. To help those businesses succeed and keep the progress moving forward, the United States solidified a free-trade agreement with Colombia. Military, business, and government working together creating sustainable gains. A model that worked. And it fit the mission.

For years, outside advisors said, "Why don't you just make the product in China like everybody else? Make huge margins, then donate a portion to a nonprofit in Afghanistan. That makes more sense on paper."

They were right. It did make more sense on paper, but it didn't create jobs and promote social change—not within the mission statement. The Colombian option helped entrepreneurs and a country affected by conflict, but there still wasn't the positive change desired in Afghanistan.

Sadly, the show ended with no booked sales or leads. The booth was packed up and shipped to a holding facility. The team returned home to Los Angeles and Issaquah to continue working.

The last remaining pairs of flip-flops pushed out of the garage. Boutique dealer sales began to reach out to us. The mission was still receiving attention in print, on TV, and on social media. People kept hitting the website, following on social media, and kept the company at a steady stream of revenue through shirt and accessory sales. It didn't look pretty on the profit and loss statement, but it was better than before and gave Andy enough time to work product development with our new Colombian partners.

By July, the first samples arrived. They were better than the initial ones we'd received from China. They were better than our failed production run, and they were definitely better than anything we made. With a few quick photos of the new flops posted to social media, the team gained affirmation from the community that the footwear was still badass. Preorders started coming in from individual buyers as well as dealers.

We appeared to be back in business.

During the summer, two major events happened. First, a Dutch dealer contacted us to purchase footwear. It was a small boutique with the theme of mission-driven products. We fit their business model, and he wanted a run of footwear. Another force multiplier for the Unarmed Forces.

Upon review of his website, a specific jewelry line stood out. The jewelry was made from unexploded ordnance leftover after the Vietnam War. The company, Article 22, was led by a recovering fashionista turned entrepreneur. They figured out how to fund landmine clearance by selling high-end jewelry made by landmines. Clever.

A quick Google search delivered the website and contact information. Without hesitation, the inquiry email went out.

```
Hi,

I saw your line of products in a store
in the Netherlands. It's cool. We're doing
something along the same lines. Would you
be open to working with us?
                        Combat Flip Flops
```

In less than a day, the response came in.

`Yes.`

Liz is the badass at the helm of Article 22. By her early thirties she'd created a global high-end jewelry line that was employing de-mining workers, supporting artist families, and arming consumers with the ability to retake terrain. She'd assembled a motivated, highly communicative, and fashionable team. A welcome ally to the Unarmed Forces.

After a few weeks of emails, the first laser-engraved bangle bracelet arrived. The "Peacemaker." Each piece sold funded the clearance of three square meters of Unexploded Ordnance (UXO) through Nobel Prize winning Mines Advisory Group (MAG).

Thanks to the United States, there is a virtually endless supply of UXO in Laos. During the Vietnam War, the United States dropped between 250,000,000 to 280,000,000 munitions on Laos in an effort to stem the flow of Viet Cong on the Ho Chi Minh Trail. To put it in scale, that's a B-52 load of munitions every eight minutes for nine years. Anything that is made by the lowest bidder, falls from a plane at a few hundred miles an hour, and impacts a jungle has a high potential of failure. It's estimated that 30,000,000 to 50,000,000 non-functioning munitions are still on the ground in Laos, covering in excess of 25% of the nation. That's one quarter of a country covered by unmarked explosives laying about. Over fifty years later, these munitions are still injuring people. They need to be cleaned up, and Liz's team was doing something about it.

They had blank inventory and could deliver quickly. This meant we had a product to push while the flip-flops were going into production. The Unarmed Forces grew to include the Article 22 team. T-shirts, hats, jewelry, and flip-flop pre-orders. Things started to look up.

Messages from the community poured in from all over the world. Articles about businesses in Africa, the Balkans, and Afghanistan. Yes. Afghanistan. It was a BBC news article and video. It stood out.

The video showed an Afghan woman, Hassina Sherjan, speaking about women's education in Afghanistan. Her message was clear. *Educate a woman and you educate a family. Educated families are prosperous and peaceful. Women's education is the key.*

Images of the schools run by her non-profit. Aid Afghanistan for Education showed little girls in white hijabs sitting in classrooms. It showed young women. It showed elderly women. They were learning to read. Since 1979, schools in Afghanistan haven't had the best environment for learning. Under the Taliban, women weren't allowed in school. Her classrooms were swollen with generations of women yearning for an education. It was inspiring.

The memory of the hillside school flashed back. Girls in school. The universe clicked all of the pieces into place. It started to make sense. If the Taliban was able to leverage uneducated youth to overthrow a government, oppress a population, and foster terrorism—would they be able to do it without uneducated youth? If the kids were educated, would the Taliban have a recruitment base? Unlikely. So how do you educate the kids? You educate the women.

Currently, literacy rates in Afghanistan are estimated at about 31% of the adult population (over the age of fifteen). Female literacy levels are, on average, 15-17% with high variation, indicating a strong geographic and gender divide. The highest female literacy rate, for instance, is 34.7%, found in the capital, Kabul, while rates as low as 1.6% are found in two southern provinces of the country. Male literacy rates average about 45%, again with high variation. The highest male literacy rates are in Kabul at 68%, while the lowest is found in Helmand at 41%.[4]

How can we expect a country to rise out of poverty, end warfare, or become an economic hub, if *MORE THAN HALF* of the population can't read? By the way, that half of the population is responsible for raising 100% of the future generation.

With another quick Google search, AAE's website produced a contact email address. In less than twenty-four hours, Hassina responded directly and requested a Skype call. We quickly began learning about each other's mission and how we could work together.

Hassina story is impressive to say the least. She's an Afghan born woman who fled to the United States with her family during the Soviet invasion. Raised and educated in the US, Hassina returned to Afghanistan after her father's

---

[4] http://www.unesco.org/new/en/kabul/education/youth-and-adult-education/enhancement-of-literacy-in-afghanistan-iii/

passing. Upon her return, she witnessed the oppressing force of the Taliban and felt compelled to act. She attempted discussions to fund schools for girls in Afghanistan but was denied. Instead, she started educating Afghan women in Pakistani refugee camps. The program grew, and after the fall of the Taliban in 2001, she returned to Afghanistan and moved her programs forward. In less than a decade, she funded thirteen schools educating nearly 3,000 women and men annually. If there's anybody on the Nobel Peace Prize nomination committee reading this book… Hint. Hint.

But she didn't stop at education. Hassina is an entrepreneur as well. Understanding that the workforce still didn't employ women, she created a factory to support women in need. They made decorative pillows, curtains, and embroidered products that were sold locally and in Europe. Jobs AND Education.

Amateurs talk tactics. Professionals talk logistics. The products previously intended to be made in Afghanistan were too expensive simply based on material sourcing and logistical costs. If a product could be made in Afghanistan and shipped directly to the US, a significant portion of the costs would be saved. There was a potential to create viable products with Hassina and her team.

During one of our Skype calls I asked, "Hassina, can you make sarongs?"

"A sarong?"

"You know. One of those beach wraps that girls wear. Could you embroider some for us to go along with our flip-flops?"

"Send some photos. I'll see what we can do."

Most flip-flop companies sell flip-flops using gratuitous bikini shots. Although the imagery is appreciated, it would be a conflicting message for a company working to help a country with a historical record of oppressing women by objectifying women. But throw a sarong on... Bam. A viable Afghan product and tasteful beach shots to help sell footwear.

Afghan production was back in business. Within a month, she delivered the first order of sarongs. Each one took ten hours to manufacture, and they were absolutely stunning. Beautifully embroidered flowers flowed down the edges of the sarong. They looked great in photos and immediately went on the website for preorders. The community responded and began to purchase.

In less than six months, production expanded to Colombia, Laos, the United States, and back to Afghanistan. A rebirth made possible only by the community, the revolutionaires, the Unarmed Forces.

Chapter VIII
-Going Beyond-

TOMS is the kingpin of the socially driven business. Their "One for One" motto and model resonates with people all over the world. Buy a pair of shoes, and they give away a pair of shoes to a person in need. It makes the consumer feel good when they buy a pair of their shoes. Because that's what you're buying, right? The feeling. In many ways, TOMS is the harbinger of the commercial exchange of a positive feeling. Every time someone slips on a pair of their footwear, it is a subtle reminder that they contributed something positive to someone in need.

The wheel works. There's no need to reinvent it; however, with a little foresight and engineering, the wheel has been improved innumerable times throughout history. The same can be said for businesses. No matter how well constructed a pair of shoes is, they have an expiry date. "Give a man a fish.." so to speak, but to teach, to give education is to give empowerment. An empowered human creates their own opportunity, their own freedom, and their own precious liberty. Education is the seed from which the tree of liberty grows.

The image of those little white hijabs reluctantly

bouncing their way to that remote schoolhouse in the Panjshir Valley visits me with ever increasing frequency. Along with the vivid image comes an inescapable, multifarious emotion. Those pesky fucking emotions, dangerous at times, driving at others. The frequency in which this particular memory returns demands an unpacking. Introspection is the key to Pandora's Box.

The guilt of having participated in the cruelty of war is persistent. An undercurrent of shame and remorse flows perpetually, subtle in the busy moments of life, raging during the quiet ones. A drop adds to that river every instance doing what is easy, popular, or "necessary" is done in favor of doing what is right. A person need not experience the depths of war to understand the friction caused by such dissonance. We are all culpable for the good we choose not to do in the world.

Why does socially driven business resonate with so many people. It can't be simply for the sake of feeling good. We can get that anywhere. Hell, a piece of chocolate can make a person feel good. The reason can't be just about balancing our negative actions, can it? Why give a fuck about someone you never met—you'll never meet—who has a problem you've never faced?

It goes beyond doing good, beyond scrubbing the residue of shame from having done bad. It goes beyond guilt, beyond altruism. It's complex, but not at all complicated. An action which contributes to the betterment of other people is a step, ascending, toward being a better human. That is why we are here.

That is an emotion, a feeling, an ethos worth packing and shipping to people all over the world.

I called Hassina with a simple idea for radical change. "Hassina, would you be open to partnering with us?"

"How?"

"For every product we sell, we fund a day of school for one of your kids?"

"Yes. Ok. That sounds terrific."

As soon as the conversation ended, Hassina's factory moved into action. Developing a manufacturing partnership from halfway around the world would have been impossible ten years ago. Thanks to the use of emails, text messages, and Skype calls, the first of many packages containing our collaborative products arrived on at my doorstep fewer than sixty days after our initial conversation.

The community showed their love for the idea every time they added one to their shopping cart. The sales machine started functioning again. By fall of 2013, the financial spreadsheets were bad, but they were trending toward breakeven. Spikes in revenue were tied to media, then fell flat for a few weeks, then spiked with a social post or news article. We needed more spikes.

I met Kate a few years prior at the Outdoor Retailer Show. At the time, she was running marketing and media for a technical outdoor company in New Hampshire. In 2013, she branched out and started her own public relations company to help small businesses interact with professional media. She was looking for new clients and offered to help. Within weeks, Kate successfully garnered more media traction for our company. Highly viewed blogs, TV news stations, and digital media. Kate was doing such a good job that it became necessary to rebuild our hastily constructed website, built in under seventy-two hours, a year and a half before. It was time to put forward a professional effort. We needed to build a brand.

Magner Sanborn, a marketing and advertising fim out of Spokane, WA was our answer. When they learned about the mission, the opportunity to fund education, and help veterans, they were in. We couldn't afford them, so they donated hours and put an intern named Mandy on the account. In less than a month, a small team put together the logo, messaging, and brand guidelines. They didn't have to, but they did. They believed in the mission.

The following year was a solid grind. Aim small. Miss small. Be creative. Make products. Have fun. Don't lose money. Make more products. Put girls in school.

By early 2015, we were trending to $300,000 in sales up from $150,000 the year previously. 100% growth. Given the previous failures we overcame, the growth was miraculous. The business began to function. We were witnessing our infant begin to walk on its own. Positive, comical, and full of hope. All made possible by those early revolutionaries.

Mandy from Magner Sanborn graduated college and moved on, but continued to volunteer her time for several more months to help drive the mission and message. A veteran lending company, Streetshares, provided a loan for inventory. Two angel investors, Sam and Sheryl, fueled the mission with enough cash to entertain a local venture capital firm, TA Group Holdings (TAG). Lead by a former Army Ranger, TAG aligned with the mission and invested. All the while Kate continued to provide media exposure.

Meeting members of the media can often go a lot of different ways. They could be a nineteen-year-old college intern majoring in Communications all the way up to a seasoned war correspondent. By early 2015, I found myself in a stream of podcasts, media interviews, and editorials. The story and mission was stated thousands of times. It was to the point where the family would cringe when they'd hear it again at a party. It was often difficult to continue preparing for each interview in between sales meetings, business calls, and packing boxes.

On a sunny February day, Lee and I crossed Ocean Park Boulevard to grab a beer and meet a reporter. We'd just finished a meeting with Activision about partnering on a product for their veteran endowment and had time for an interview before the evening flight back to Seattle. Kate was insistent we meet this writer named Wes. She went on about how big of a deal he is, how he wrote for *Jalopnik* and *Playboy*. He's a huge blogger with a big following...Yeah. Yeah. Yeah.

So this guy rolled up on a shiney hipster motorcycle wearing a leather jacket and pulled off his helmet to reveal the most dapper human I think either of us had ever seen. Standing 6'1" with a fit build, he sauntered up to us confidently. "You Griff?"

"Yes."

"Let's grab a beer."

All three of us saddled up to the bar. It was the typical small talk to start, then he set his phone on the bar between our beers and asked, "You mind if I record this?"

"Sure, man."

The next twenty minutes consisted of the standard tale. About halfway through, Wes's posture changed. He began asking questions and cracking jokes. The exchange ranged from motorcycles to the outdoors to the mission. He reminded me of the meeting with John years ago in Kabul. At some point in the conversation I interrupted, "Hey Wes."

"What?"

"Weird knows weird. You don't know this yet, but we're gonna be friends."

The look on his face conveyed a mix of relief, fear, and curiosity. Then the conversation picked back up, all the way to the bottom of the beer. After his last sip, he set the glass down, picked up his phone, and spun on his barstool to say, "I gotta roll, guys. I need to catch a jet to Vegas to party with Billy Idol."

What? Billy Idol? Vegas?

And he was off on his hipster bike, zipping through Santa Monica. Lee and I hopped in his FJ Cruiser and headed to LAX. Back to the grind in the garage.

Home-based businesses present a lot of challenges. When your desk is fifteen feet from the living room, it's difficult to not check email, answer calls, or compulsively look at web traffic and sales numbers during family time. In an effort to create separation between home life and work life, the computer and desk moved into the garage. With the glue smell aired out and the boxes gone, it was suitable as an office space. No windows. No insulation. Just lights, production tables, power outlets, and a space heater.

The following Tuesday after meeting Wes, at roughly 3:00 p.m. Pacific Standard Time, our website crashed. I was attempting to adjust inventory on the admin side while Lee was trying to test product links. The site was dead. Text messages flew back and forth between me and Lee.

> Lee, the site's down. Get that shit fixed.

> Dude. Are you seeing all these sales leading up the the crash?

> What sales?

I hit the home button on the iPhone. Hit the Mail app. Proceeded to thumb scroll through hundreds of orders.

> What the fuck happened?

> That *Gizmodo* article hit.

> *Gizmodo*?

> Wes. That guy we met with last week. His article just posted on *Gizmodo,* and it's crushing traffic.

Can you get the website back up?

I'm on the support line with GoDaddy right now.

Over 100,000 people read the most rational, well-articulated, and motivating article anybody had ever written about the mission. Wes crushed it. Hundreds of people left thoughtful and enduring comments, creating a discussion which continued on the site for weeks. The dialogue was free of trolling, arguing, or otherwise ugly behavior— a truly unique and welcome departure from most internet conversations. The positive, respectful, and fruitful conversation drove the largest spike in traffic and sales in company history. We immediately went into backorder status and scrambled to get production rolling. Major retailers began to call. It was an exponential expansion of the Unarmed Forces.

Kate deserves a slow clap for that one.

Chapter IX
- Surfing with Sharks -

There are certain moments, opportunities, in life and in business alike which carry the potential to alter one's path irrevocably. They seem to present themselves from the ether. The truth is those opportunities have a solid foundation cast in the mortar and stone of hard work and preparation. The art, the nuance of success, is recognizing that moment for what it is when it flashes in front of you, and then being fearless enough to grab it confidently, without concern of repercussion or consequence.

Six weeks after the *Gizmodo* article was published, one of those moments came ringing a little before midnight. The caller ID read, "Culver City, CA"

Who calls at 11:30 p.m.?

Apparently executive producers of television shows. His name is Max, and within thirty seconds of the call, I knew we were going to be friends. He was engaging, with a calm energy, and yet a noticeable enthusiasm emanated in the tone of his voice.

He presented an offer, an opportunity...

"Shark Tank."

"I don't know man. Shark Tank is the American Idol for young entrepreneurs. I don't watch much TV, but from what I've seen of the show, you get ratings by destroying entrepreneurs who haven't put in the work yet."

"I get it, but I think Combat Flip Flops would be perfect for the show."

"I don't know."

"I'm going to send you the application packet now. Fill it out and get back to me."

"Ok. I'll check it out."

In less than five minutes, the word document sat as an attachment in my inbox. Compartmentalization learned in the military transferred into the business mindset. No excitement. No waking up the wife to let her know. Just hit CTRL+T and drop it in the task list.

The following morning, Andy, Lee, and I went through the daily priorities during the morning conference call. At the bottom of the list toward the end of the call I let them know about the offer from the night prior.

"Oh yeah, one more thing. I got a call from a producer at Shark Tank last night. They read the *Gizmodo* article and want us to apply to be on the show."

"What?" Lee enthusiastically interrupts.

"Yeah. He called super late. I told him that we'd need to talk about it, but unlikely we'd apply."

"ARE YOU FUCKING HIGH? DO YOU KNOW HOW MANY PEOPLE WATCH THAT SHOW?"

Andy chimes in, "What Lee said."

"Fill out that application right now."

The team had voted. Apparently, the time had come to to jump into the water with Sharks. There were no stipulations on how I should fill out the application, but I was gripped by feelings of hesitation. Nothing a beer or two wouldn't solve. After dinner that evening, I disappeared into the garage with a six'r of the Northwest's finest, Rainier, opened the email attachment and got to work.

The document consisted of six or seven pages of questions. Each question had six or seven lines for typed or handwritten answers. It was tough to imagine the courage it took for business owners to fill it out in hopes of broadcasting their dreams in front of millions of viewers, with the complete and total possibility of crushing or getting crushed in front of America. The liquid courage loosened my fingers and the typing comensed. My responses were short, to the point, and rarely made it to the end of the second line, at best. Before midnight, I sent the completed Word document back to Max.

Another call from Culver City displayed on the caller ID early the next morning.

As soon as I answered, I heard Max's enthusiastic voice, "Dude. This is great."

"Really?"

"Yeah. Best application we've seen in a while. Can you assemble an application video for us? No. Wait. Scratch that. There's enough of your stuff on Youtube. I'll get it put together and push it past the team. Expect to get an email from our associate producers soon."

"You're kidding, right?"

Max was not kidding. Two months later, at 11:00 p.m. I lay awake in a hotel room, mentally grappling with the prospect of the most important meeting in the company's history. In twelve hours, Lee and I will go on camera in front of 11,000,000 people to pitch five of the most influential and successful entrepreneurs in the country that America's longest war can and should be won with flip-flops. There were a lot more than just dollars on the line.

Thoughts of the company's reputation, of my reputation, of jobs, and education all ricocheted inside my head. Lee seemed at ease with the crucible ahead. He'd been snoring aggressively for an hour in the bed next to mine. The sounds Lee makes while he sleeps are almost as legendary as his barista skills. Somehow he manages to sleep through his throat making a sound that resembles a bear getting mauled by a chainsaw. It's a sound I'm familiar with. After years of sharing sleeping quarters with Lee, I'd worked out a system. I take all of his pillows from his bed except the one he's using. Over the course of the night, I toss them at him every time he revs up the saw.

Tonight I had a backup plan as well. To drown out the snoring, I threw my earbuds in and hit a recent mix on SoundCloud. Maybe I could distract myself from the nervousness and fear with some beats. The crappy reading light illuminated the spreadsheets which covered bed. Sales forecasts. Profit and loss statements. Cash flow. Multiple permutations of each to reflect breakeven, forecasted increase, and scale. 8.5x11 sheets of printer paper held the same numbers.

Repetition. Repetition. Repetition of the fundamentals. It's the reason Rangers lead the way. Flash won't get you there. Success is a mastery of the basics, preparation, and an ability to adjust fire without hesitation. When we stepped into that meeting tomorrow, nothing would be left to chance.

Layed over the top of a savory reggae beat, a musical mantra of sorts flowed into my consciousness.

"Nothing gets accomplished with a focus on fear."

As if it was meant to be. At the right time. In the right moment. The perfect lyrics. He was right. Nothing gets accomplished with a focus on fear.

I'd been through two wars, multiple other hot spots, nearly died a handful of times, been broke and heartbroken. What had I learned from all of those experiences?

Be present. Focus. Slow down. See the win. Put everything you have into creating the reality you desire. Nothing gets accomplished with a focus on fear.

And the sleep came easy.

The carpet felt unsettling under my feet. Some strange mix of plush, industrial berber, atop a concrete floor. Smooth and squishy all at the same time—we'd only rehearsed on concrete or hardwood floors. No matter how many things you plan for, variables vary. That carpet lead right to a pair of big, brown wood doors. Plastic plants lined long tables adjacent to the doors. A cameraman, a makeup artist, Max, Lee, and I all occupied the small room.

The emotions were high, but we'd survived much worse. Had this been twelve years prior, that door would be a mere obstacle between us and the objective. There would be a team of Rangers stacked up behind the hinges, explosives placed with precision, and dual primers in the hand of a man about to do dangerous work. There is a frenzied calm in these moments. A clarity. A focus. A flow. Strategic compartmentalization of emotions enables focus on the fundamentals of winning. Today, however, wasn't about timing of helicopters and gunships—it was story, math, and smiles. The sweat was already boiling up on both our brows, but we knew the calm was coming.

The makeup lady hovered over Lee. Some guy to our left wearing one of those full body camera rigs stood three feet to my right. A sound technician fondled my butt while dropping the remote mic onto my belt.

Max is what you would imagine of a Hollywood professional. Five foot eight, cool black classes, neatly trimmed jet black hair in a professionally messy arrangement. Cool jeans, sneakers, and old button-down shirt.

Max makes a last-second suggestion. "Guys, I've been thinking about it. I really think you should up your valuation."

Lee gives me his standard, *What do you think?* look. It wasn't the plan. We'd made it to this moment in part by a series of coin flips, shakes of the Magic 8-Ball, and rock, paper, scissors. I didn't have any change or the 8-Ball. Rock, paper, scissors it is.

The makeup lady, dressed in Hollywood black, aggressively

assaulted the sweat beads descending my forehead with that weird triangle sponge.

"OK, Max. We'll rock, paper, scissors for it."

"Are you fucking serious?"

The makeup lady stalls, mouth open, and stares at my right hand curled into a fist above my flat left palm.

"Yeah, man. One shake. On three. Ready?"

Max was up for it. Paper beats rock. I lose.

"All right then, $300,000 for 10% it is." I concluded.

That's a $3,000,000 valuation for a company working toward $300,000 in revenue. Ten times revenue. Totally unreasonable and likely to be laughed at by any venture capital investor. The standard for any high-growth company operating at break even or a loss is three to five times revenue. We're going to get bent over on national TV.

Makeup complete. Butt fondling ceased. Camera still hovering in the periphery. Max was gone. Just Lee and I now. One more mission. We turned toward the door.

The moment felt like we were once again stepping into the back of a C-130 together. With the weight of armor around our necks, minds focused on the objective, we exchanged our habitual parting words.

"Well, Lee, everybody wants to be a gangster until it's time to do gangster shit."

"You drive. I steer. We got this."

"One minute," somebody said from behind us.

There was no getting off this ride. Last second mental cycles of operation procedures, malfunction drills, and visualization. Eighteen paces from the first door to the second. Eight paces from the second door to the mark. Hold. Thirty second hold while the cameras film the products. Then game time.

"30 seconds."

We'd watched it hundreds of times with family. Cheered. Booed. Speculated. Now we were up. We were going to destroy this objective. Ahh. The calm.

"Go."

The oversized wood doors opened automatically in front of us. Commence pace count.

"Are those TV screens? Not Aquariums? Weird.

Fourteen...fifteen...sixteen. The second set of doors opened. There they were. All five of them lined up. Business leaders held in the highest regard.

Billionaire Maverick Mark Cuban on the left, messing with his cell phone. Daymond John to his right looking over a piece of paper. Kevin O'Leary known ironically as "Mr. Wonderful" in the center. On the right, Lori Greiner and Robert Herjavec whispering to one another.

Be present. Focus. Make ready.

Everyone knows the music. *Da-da-da-da. DUM DUM. DUM DUM.* The tune set the tone for what was to come. The only problem was, there was no music. The studio was distractingly silent.

What? There's no music? I wonder if Lee is thinking the same thing too? Hey, Mr. Wonderful is doing that fingers touching thing in front of his face. Damn, Cuban is really tall. Is his chair lower than Lori's to make them look even on TV? The lack of dramatic music is really distracting me. Ok. Focus. Back to work.

A voice from our left shouts "Go" one more time.

We'd spent two months refining this pitch. Over and over and over and over again. Starting outside the garage doors, swinging them open, walking in, and delivering. We discussed the details with the associate producers on video calls every Tuesday at 11:00 a.m. We rehearsed right up to the the night prior in our hotel room. Lee and I walked back and forth between the double beds to the exact pace count, had a timer for the thirty second hold, and delivered.

Preparation. Mastery of the fundamentals. The pitch went as expected. Lee crushed his lines. We were so excited that the initial delivery went so well that the sharks just stared at us. We stared back. A full stall.

Cuban seemed annoyed, "Well, are you guys going to show us the product or what?"

Caught up in the moment, we forgot everything after the pitch. Mr. Cuban snapped us back to reality. Now onto the good stuff—product, story, and numbers. The product was solid. The story behind the product couldn't be any better. But the numbers…

The numbers don't lie. They tell the story of a viable business. Now it was a matter of convincing the Sharks to come to the same conclusion.

Our primary targets were Lori, Daymond, and Robert.

Lori Greiner, known as the Queen of QVC, once sold more than 2,000,000 sponges in a single day by harnessing the power of television-based home-shopping.

Daymond John is a scrappy guerrilla marketer known for fashion branding. He started FUBU with a loan from his mother, which I'm sure he has since payed back in full.

Robert Herjavec is a tech ninja who fled communist oppression in Croatia with $20 in his pocket and immigrated to North America. He started off selling vacuums in Canada, turning that twenty dollars into over $200,000,000.

Kevin O'Leary. From our pre-show research, we understood him to be a stellar business partner with a tough-guy attitude for the camera. Every time we heard him say, "You're dead to me," all we heard was, "Please mess with me."

Mark Cuban is the wild card. The Maverick. We really had no idea what his interests, if any, would be in our company.

Despite the pedigree, product, story, and numbers, Kevin was the first to bow out. One might think this would be cause for concern or possibly derail our enthusiasm. Truth be told, I'd spent the months leading up to filming thinking about how to mess with Kevin on the show. He'd thrown smoke on so many of the show's guests, and it just felt right to throw some back.

Two weeks prior to filming, I shot out of bed after a particularly intense recurring dream from my time in Iraq. In a haze, I said it aloud so I wouldn't forget, then wrote it down on my journal next to the bed.

Red Chemlight

It is difficult to appreciate the chaos symphony of a midnight Ranger raid unless you've been there. It's obviously dark. There are good people intermixed among bad people everywhere. Shots fly in multiple directions.

These objectives are often confusing. The fighting has a tendency to poor out into a field or into a street. When an opponent falls, things don't stop. You have to secure the entire objective. But what about the guy on the ground? What if he's the primary target? It doesn't matter. Secure the objective first, then deal with the details. In the name of safety and expediency, a red chemlight indicates the guy on the ground is no longer in play. When you crack that red chemlight, somebody's dead, and Kevin was about to be dead to us. The last decision to make was, "Which one of us gets to kill Kevin?"

As mentioned earlier, the majority of decisions made by Combat Flip Flops comes from one of three methods: coin toss, Magic 8-Ball, or rock, paper, scissors. The day before the show, I'd lost the toss to determine which one of us got to "Kill Kevin." The words, "I'm out," rolled off Kevin's lips. The light was shining off his head as he sat back in his chair and did that weird, fingers pressed together thing in front of his face like an evil villain in a bad 80s movie.

Lee is a brother, friend, family. Outside of family, our relationship is the longest lasting I've ever had. We've been through it all together. War. Death. Marriage. Childbirth. Transition. Business. We can damn near finish each other's sentences. As we looked at one another, the mental conversation went like this.

Lee: *"Dude, did he just go out first?"*

Griff: *"Yeah, bro. This is gold."*

Lee: *"I'm so much better at rock, paper, scissors than you."*

Griff: *"Yes… you're so much better. Quit messing around and go deliver."*

Lee: *"Ok. Ok. Ok. Hold my beer."*

Lee produced the chemlight from his rear pocket, snapped the activation tab, and gave it a good shake before handing it to Mr. Wonderful in it's beautifully illuminated form.

Kevin was perplexed. "What's this?"

"It's how we mark the dead." Lee said it so casually with that cavalier smile.

The move grabbed Cuban and John's attention. They were immediately reengaged in the meeting. Lori couldn't stop smiling that somebody actually got Kevin to shut up. She joked that she may invest just for that reason alone. Robert continued quietly taking notes. The back-and-forth continued.

Prior to stepping out into the tank, we set our upper and lower thresholds. Enter at $1.5 million valuation. Take a deal with one or multiple sharks with a valuation over $750,000. If you have any shark hooked on the line between those numbers, land them, and get the bounce as quickly as possible.

Mark and Daymond were first to make a proposal at $100,000 each. A quick bit of mental math puts the valuation at $800,000. We're already in our bracket. Then Lori chimes in. The mission needed a feminine touch, and we made it clear to Cuban and John. The banter between the three of them began.

Three sharks means they'll want more of the business. We planned for this only as a longshot. If they want more of the business, the mission would need more cash.

We'd smacked Kevin so badly all he could do was moderate the investment discussion. He teed it up perfectly. "Would you do a deal with three sharks for 30%? That's a lot of horsepower."

A million. It just sounds good. A million dollar idea.

"Three hundred for thirty?" The numbers rolled off my tongue with ease.

Quick head nods and affirmations of the sharks. "Deal."

Handshakes, hugs, gratitude to Kevin and Robert for listening. About face. Exit quickly. We bagged three high value targets, now get off the X. We can do the emotion thing later.

Six months later, the operations center was set. A long boardroom table lined with laptops focused on a big screen hanging on the wall. The dashboard was set. Onsite traffic, revenue, email registrations. The ranks of Unarmed Forces were about to swell. People all of the world were about to go to work in an effort to manufacture peace through trade. We knew we were about to send a lot of little girls to school.

Family, investors, friends, and customers showed up and lined the hallway outside of the boardroom. The energy was unbelievably positive. We'd held the results closely with anybody outside the immediate family and investors.

All lights started to flash green across the dashboard. "The Shark Tank Effect" was in full swing. Our team was humming on social media, website inventory, and sabering bottles of champagne. As a team, we'd nurtured this idea from infancy. We watched now, proud parents, as she took center stage and blossomed into adulthood before our eyes.

In thirty-six hours, sales eclipsed all total revenue in the company's history. The email list increased by tens of thousands. Purchase orders started moving products into motion. The days of school ticked up. In a day and a half, the swelling ranks of the Unarmed Forces funded the education of over 200 girls in Afghanistan for an entire year.

Moments of clarity came between cheers, smiles, and phone calls. There were roughly 20 girls in hijabs headed toward that school outside the Panjshir valley. This one television appearance meant ten times that many throughout Afghanistan would have an education. From an idea, to paper, to digital rendering, to sample, to production, through multiple failures, and raised from the ashes—the Unarmed Forces moved forward—creating the change we all desire.

Like proud parents, we cried a lot. The immense gratitude for those who supported the mission was overwhelming. The Unarmed Forces started with a handful of steadfast believers and has since advanced the mission to fund education for over 600 children (as of Summer 2018). Factories rebuilt, jobs created, a generation of little girls elevated using a sustainable model without a single casualty (other than Kevin).

The book in your hands funded another day of education for a little girl in Afghanistan. You funded an opportunity for empowerment and helped to create a better human, and you're a better human for it. Thank you.

You've likely noticed this is the final passage. That, however, does not mean we are at the end of the story. Quite the contrary. This is the beginning, the rise. This has simply been your indoctrination into the Unarmed Forces. You are a member now, a willing participant in a mission to rectify an imbalance and empower the oppressed. We will go forth together. And together we will be a better human.

Welcome to the Unarmed Forces.

About the Authors

Matthew "Griff" Griffin graduated the United States Military Academy in 2001 before accepting a commission into the Field Artillery. Between 2003-2005, Griff deployed four times to Iraq and Afghanistan with 2d Ranger Battalion as a Company Fire Support Officer. After departing the military in 2006, Griff worked in the defense sector which eventually led him back to Afghanistan to assist with medical infrastructure development. After witnessing the positive effects of economic growth in conflict areas, Griff co-founded Combat Flip Flops with a fellow Ranger and began the mission to manufacture peace through trade. He was recognized in 2017 as one of the top 100 Most Influential Veterans in America and in 2018 as a top 100 Global Visionary.

Leo Jenkins served multiple deployments to Afghanistan and Iraq as a US Army Ranger medic in support of the Global War on Terrorism. He is the acclaimed author of Lest We Forget: A Ranger Medic's Story, On Assimilation: A Return From War, First Train out of Denver, With a Pen, and coauthor of Violence of Action: The Untold Stories of the 75th Ranger Regiment in the War on Terror. He studied International relations with a focus on terrorism and political violence at Indiana University and Purdue University and has traveled through over fifty countries in pursuit of a deeper understanding of the human condition.

G.H

206 5525500

Text me

griff@combatflipflops.com

Made in the USA
Monee, IL
18 March 2020

23447179R10101